November 8 2018

MW00979759

TRUE RIGHT

Genuine Conservative Leaders of Western Canada

BY MICHAEL WAGNER

Author Michael Wagner is one of Canada's unsung heroes, a man who publishes book after well-researched book for the single purpose of reminding Canadian conservatives that they still have "a future and a hope" in spite of the left's all-too-apparent advantages. *True Right: Genuine Conservative Leaders of Western Canada*, is a follow on from his earlier works, most especially *Standing on Guard for Thee: The Past, Present and Future of Canada's Christian Right*. The same point is made in both books, namely that true conservatism, with its Christian roots, is native to Canada and seminal for Canada's government and ethos. In fact, as Wagner has proven in other works, Christian conservatism is *the* foundation of all that has made Canada great and prosperous. This book is a fantastic addition to Wagner's oeuvre because it delineates the leading western Canadian conservative voices of the twentieth century, examines their political thought and impact, and demonstrates conclusively that without western conservatism Canada would long ago have drowned its distinctive culture in the slough of Old World socialism.

That is the first half of the book. But the second half, in which Wagner examines the thinking and writing of Ted and Link Byfield, father and son and, respectively, founder and publisher of *Alberta Report Newsmagazine*, is perhaps his book's most important contribution toward strengthening the foundation of conservative thought. Full disclosure: it was my privilege to serve as a senior editor and, toward the magazine's end in 2003, managing editor of *Alberta Report*. Nevertheless, I insist that one can argue objectively that through their columns, written either for their magazine or published elsewhere, the Byfields were Canada's preeminent conservative prophets and teachers. They predicted and explained the current breakdown of society two decades ago, and then went on to prescribe the necessary, though presently unpopular curatives. Wagner's sterling achievement has been to distill and present to his readers the pure essence of their thinking on the relevant issues of our time. One feels that no one can read this material without being inspired to pray and, one hopes, to work for the day when conservatism once more guides the nation.

– Shafer Parker, Jr., Pastor, Hawkwood Baptist Church, Calgary, and former Senior Editor of *Alberta Report* magazine.

Feeling like you're the last true conservative left in Justin Trudeau's Canada? You need to read Michael Wagner's *True Right* and find out that all through Canada's history great, solid, courageous conservative men have stood up to the socialist hordes. Wagner presents short biographies of 17 political leaders who shaped Western Canada, and explains why some were true conservatives and some weren't. There's controversy to be had in the "weren't" camp, where Wagner places some big and well-loved names...but his reasoning is hard to argue with. Among the 13 "were"s most readers will find a pleasant surprise or two, meeting stalwart gentlemen who they'd not previously known. What an encouragement to hear that we're not alone! Yes, even in Canada there have always been true conservatives, good and godly men, who were willing to stand up and fight, win or lose.

– Jon Dykstra, Editor, *Reformed Perspective* magazine

Michael has assiduously outlined several Canadian politicians and writers who have looked, albeit imperfectly, to the Bible to inform their social conservatism, and to limited government and the rule of law to lessen the effects of fallen man in the economic and political realms. Learn about several impactive Western Canadian leaders and then stand on their shoulders to lead Canada in the direction of what Michael calls "Byfield conservatism." Share this book widely with your friends and teach the crisp and inspiring biographies it contains to the next generation.

– Ted Tederoff, Past President, Alberta Home Education Association

Book Summary:

Canadian conservatives need to know about the past heroes of their movement. They also need to know about the thought leaders who inspired many to understand and act upon the truths that conservatism represents. Out west, at least, many Canadians have favoured limited government, free enterprise and traditional morality going back many decades. This is the perspective of genuine conservatism. And it is a heritage that needs to be understood and embraced as the ideological foundation of true Canadian conservatism for current and future generations.

A central purpose of this book is to highlight western Canadian conservative leaders, their perspectives and accomplishments, as a basis for encouraging and inspiring Canadians to embrace this legacy of genuine conservatism. As well, a basic outline of "Byfield conservatism" is sketched, followed by a more detailed consideration of the political thought of Link and Ted Byfield. Byfield conservatism is a true and indigenous Canadian conservatism. It is this form of conservatism that will need to thrive if Canada is to be rescued from its current destructive course.

Bio:

Michael Wagner is the author of *Standing on Guard for Thee: The Past, Present and Future of Canada's Christian Right* and *Alberta: Separatism Then and Now*. He has a PhD in Political Science from the University of Alberta and lives in Edmonton with his wife and eleven children.

Freedom Press Canada Inc
12-111 Fourth Ave. , Suite 185
St. Catharines, ON L2S 3P5

Cover design: David Bolton

Book design: David Bolton

Printed in the USA

ISBN: 978-1-927684-41-2

DEDICATION

To Vince Byfield,

who continues to carry the torch

ACKNOWLEDGEMENTS

I am very grateful to Susan Hearn
for her continued support of my research and writing.

Contents

FOREWORD

It is easy for Christians to lapse into despair over politics and the seemingly endless march by all parties towards the "centre," which to most of us is decidedly non-Christian, amoral and more bewildering with each new cause. I confess I'm a cynic, despite decades of writing, thinking and talking about politics and being repeatedly disappointed by people and parties in which I vested considerable hope and energy.

It was good for me to read Michael Wagner's *True Right* to be reminded of the many good western Canadian politicians who worked very hard to govern without abandoning their Christian principles and beliefs.

The biographies are important: not only do they remind us of the achievements of the individual politicians, but they highlight the cultural shift over the decades. Alberta Premier Ernest Manning could run the province *and* preach weekly to a national radio audience on Back to the Bible Hour. This is unthinkable today unless the "preacher" avoided commenting on most of the Ten Commandments.

It's more difficult for me to assess the second part of this book on the "Byfield conservatism." I worked for the *Alberta Report* and associated magazines for 25 of the 30-year run. I think there is little doubt that the political ideas set forth had a very direct impact on Alberta politics and in turn, national politics in this country. It was a driving force in the creation and promotion of the Reform Party. The 1987 Western Assembly in Vancouver, which drew hundreds of Westerners and led to the establishment of the party, was almost entirely ignored by the media, except *Alberta Report*. Ted Byfield was a speaker at the event and we had several others in attendance covering the assembly. Michael Wagner documents this influence on both the provincial and federal fronts.

Of more interest, perhaps, to Christians, are the writings of Link and Ted on the moral questions of the day. I was struck by the prescience of some of these passages written years ago. Many accused them and the magazine of extreme positions and dramatic overstatement of the effects of changes in laws and practices. The critics were so wrong, then and now. You see, to plagiarize (and correct) a long-time political theme: "It's the culture, stupid." The *Report* magazines and the Byfields talked politics a lot, but their real strength was influencing the culture, that being, conservative and Christian.

I hope that *True Right* informs, reminds and inspires. Religion and politics are uneasy, but necessary, partners. We cannot live our faith while ignoring how we are governed. *True Right* helps us to see where we've been and how our faith is crucial to a healthy political culture.

Joanne Byfield
Edmonton, Alberta

PREFACE

During the summer and fall months of 2013, Freedom Press Canada had a webpage for articles written by Canadian conservatives. It was called Freedom Press Journal and one new article was added each weekday. I began contributing articles, usually about important figures in western Canadian conservativism.

After some of these had appeared, the site's editor, Professor Janice Fiamengo, emailed me to say that she and Freedom Press president Tristan Emmanuel had discussed the possibility of compiling my articles into a book about western Canadian conservatism. They apparently shared my view that Canadian conservatives would benefit by learning about political leaders (and other notable figures) that represented a genuine conservative perspective in our country. I liked the idea, but I was extremely busy and the project was shelved for a couple of years.

It wasn't until the fall of 2015 that work really began on this project. As well, a considerable amount of additional material needed to be produced to make it viable. This led to a significant expansion of the "Byfield conservatism" segment as well as additional chapters on notable people or events in western Canadian conservatism.

In my view, as someone who has spent much of my life intensely interested in conservatism, the Byfields stand out for their depth of thoughtfulness about, and personal devotion to, genuine conservatism. I think

"Byfield conservatism" is the truest expression of western Canadian conservatism.

History is very important, much more important than most people realize. The Byfields know this better than anyone, and it led to their creation of a multi-volume history of Alberta and a multi-volume history of Christianity. Much of this book is also history. Hopefully home-grown conservative heroes can become recognized so that Canadian conservatives don't always have to look abroad for leaders to admire. Margaret Thatcher and Ronald Reagan are great people and worthy of esteem, but we've had good people here too, despite their smaller jurisdictions and lower profiles.

There is much more than history here. The principles underlying the political thought of Link and Ted Byfield are not just museum pieces to be studied as history. The principles they expounded are enduring and point the way towards a better future.

It is my hope that this book can contribute to a better future by reminding western Canadian conservatives of their heritage and the principles of a genuine indigenous political perspective. As the conclusion argues, a better future can only be achieved by a return to God.

INTRODUCTION

My first course in political science at the University of Calgary over thirty years ago was very depressing. I was self-consciously right-wing in my political views but I was taught that Canada basically had no genuine free enterprise or limited government political tradition. Conservatism, Liberalism and Socialism all had a presence in this country, but there wasn't much to distinguish one from the other.

Canadian Conservatism, I was taught, consisted of the "Red Tory" position. That is, it was a derivation of the British Conservative tradition that favoured a large and powerful role for the government in running society and the economy. Red Tories believed in Big Government.

Then there was Canadian Liberalism, which was primarily a variant of "Reform Liberalism." That is, it was a modern form of liberalism that favoured a large and powerful role for the government in running society and the economy. Canadian Liberals believed in Big Government.

Canadian Socialism, like socialism everywhere, favoured a large and powerful role for the government in running society and the economy. Canadian Socialists, of course, believed in Big Government.

In other words, all three major Canadian ideological perspectives considered Big Government to be the key to prosperity and stability. Only looney "far right" American ideologues believed that free enterprise and limited government offered a compelling alternative to statist policies. And those guys were considered to be just a front for the greedy capitalists who wanted greater riches at the expense of everyone else.

Gad Horowitz

This characterization is not much of an exaggeration of what I heard. In that first political science class we spent considerable time discussing the famous theory of University of Toronto political economist Gad Horowitz, which by that time had become a sort of orthodoxy in Canadian political science.

In his description of Canadian Conservatism, Horowitz noted the following: "The tory and socialist minds have some crucial assumptions, orientations, and values in common, so that from certain angles they may appear not as enemies, but as two different expressions of the same basic ideological outlook" (Horowitz 1983, 135). That is, Canadian Conservatism shared "the same basic ideological outlook" as socialism. In the Canadian context, therefore, in many respects there was little to distinguish Conservatism from socialism.

The situation was similar with Canadian Liberalism. According to Horowitz, Canadian Liberalism emphasized its similarity to socialism as a way of attracting support. He described the perspective of Canadian Liberalism this way: "Social reform, yes; extension of public ownership, yes; the welfare state, yes; increased state control of the economy, yes; but not too much" (Horowitz 1983, 138). In other words, Canadian Liberalism was just a watered-down version of socialism.

Again, from this authoritative perspective, the three Canadian political ideologies amounted to three variations of socialism. It may be relatively softcore socialism or hardcore socialism, but it was all socialism. In short, all true Canadians were socialists, even the "Conservatives."

Horowitz was probably suffering from a bad case of Marxism which sees socialism as the inevitable outcome of history. But Marxism is based on fairy-tales, and Horowitz's characterization of Canadian ideologies contained more than a little wishful thinking on his part.

Nevertheless, as a young and impressionable undergraduate, this reigning orthodoxy was very depressing. I was Canadian born and raised, and here in my first political science class I was being taught that the political perspective I embraced didn't really exist in my own country. I wasn't even a softcore socialist, so my views were supposedly beyond the pale. But I was too young and naive to realize that I was being fed what might be called "academic bullshit."

Western Canadian Conservatism

Canada is a very large country and each region has distinctive features to its history and outlook. This is most obviously the case with Quebec, which is, in fact, a distinct society.

The political history of western Canada also differs from the rest of the country in terms of the ideological orientation of some successful politicians and governments. That is, there have been provincial governments in each of the four western provinces that were guided by a conservatism that differed substantially from the kind of so-called "Conservatism" described by Gad Horowitz. As well, for many years the West had an influential newsmagazine (first *Alberta Report*, then also *Western Report* and *BC Report*) which offered a distinctively western Canadian vision of genuine conservatism.

It is interesting to note that the Reform Party of Canada represented this same distinctively western vision of conservatism and experienced electoral success only in the four western provinces. There were party members in the central and eastern provinces as well, but the Reform Party always remained an essentially western party. That is why some felt it had to be discarded in an effort to produce a new national party, the Canadian Alliance.

A Genuine Conservative Heritage

It is important for Canadian conservatives in all parts of the country to understand that genuine, home-grown Canadian conservatism is not a softcore version of socialism as some academics have contended. Nor is it a foreign import, any more than the other political ideologies in this country. Out west, at least, many Canadians have favoured limited government, free enterprise and traditional morality going back many decades. This is the perspective of genuine conservatism. And it is a heritage that needs to be understood and embraced as the ideological foundation of true Canadian conservatism for current and future generations of conservatives.

In determining who constitutes a "genuine conservative," support for limited government, free enterprise and traditional morality are the main criteria. It is important to note, however, that some of the leaders discussed here governed in the period before the "culture war" over traditional morality came to the fore. Thus their support for traditional morality cannot be proven in a particular political debate. In the end, however,

I can't claim to have a scientific measurement process for determining the authenticity of conservatism among political leaders, and thus there is an obvious element of subjective judgment when I produce a list of genuine conservatives.

A central purpose of this book is to highlight western Canadian conservative leaders, their perspectives and accomplishments, as a basis for encouraging and inspiring Canadians to embrace this legacy of genuine conservatism. The efforts of these leaders demonstrate that small-government conservatism is native to this country and offers a better alternative than the soft socialist and hard socialist policies of other ideological perspectives.

Book Outline

This book is divided into two parts. The first part primarily consists of brief biographical accounts of important Western conservative political leaders. Many of these men have been forgotten but they should be better known among Canada's conservatives. Some of these short bios were the original basis for the book. As with all elected leaders, their actual accomplishments fell short of their conservative intentions.

A few leaders with conservative credentials, but who (in my judgment) fall short of the designation of "genuine conservative," are also discussed.

Part 2 is more philosophical because it goes into detail about "Byfield conservatism." The basic outline of Byfield conservatism is sketched and then the political thought of Link and Ted Byfield is considered in more detail. It is my view that Byfield conservatism is a true and indigenous Canadian conservatism. It is this form of conservatism that will need to thrive if our country is to be rescued from its current destructive course.

PART 1

CHAPTER 1

PREMIER ERNEST MANNING OF ALBERTA

It may be hard to imagine today, but Canada's second-longest serving premier of all time was a self-identified fundamentalist Christian. Ernest Manning (1908-1996) was premier of Alberta from 1943 to 1968. He was also a radio preacher throughout his premiership and beyond. That is, he was not a "closet Christian," but was well-known throughout the country for his conservative religious views and radio evangelism.

Ernest Manning was a Saskatchewan farm boy in the early twentieth century. As a teenager he became a Christian through the radio ministry of William "Bible Bill" Aberhart of Calgary. Manning moved to Calgary to attend Aberhart's new Bible College, the Calgary Prophetic Bible Institute, in 1927. He was the college's first graduate and became Aberhart's closest associate and right-hand man in the ministry.

Aberhart was an influential figure in Alberta by the 1920s. He taught a popular Bible class and was a respected high school principal. The main source of his influence, however, was his radio ministry, which broadcast in much of Alberta and also into parts of Saskatchewan.

Alberta was severely affected by the Great Depression that began in 1929. In searching for an answer to that economic crisis, Aberhart stumbled upon a new theory known as "Social Credit," which had been developed by a British engineer named C. H. Douglas. Social Credit was a confusing theory that combined some aspects of genuine economics with significant errors about money creation.

Unfortunately, the creator of Social Credit also held some anti-Semitic views, believing that the world was in the grasp of greedy bankers led by Jews. However, neither Aberhart nor Manning embraced the anti-Semitic aspects of Douglas's views. As sociologist Edward Bell writes, "the two Alberta men accepted Social Credit monetary theories, but did not incorporate Douglas's anti-Semitism into their beliefs or political platform" (Bell 2004, 151). In later years, Manning actively purged anti-Semites from the Social Credit movement in Alberta.

With his new theory in hand, Aberhart used his radio platform to introduce Albertans to Social Credit as a solution to their economic problems. Many people became convinced.

The Alberta Social Credit Party was formed and won the 1935 provincial election in a landslide. Aberhart became premier and appointed Manning to the cabinet. At 27 years old, Manning was the youngest cabinet minister in the British Parliamentary family since William Pitt in 1782.

Because banking and monetary affairs are in the federal jurisdiction, the numerous attempts of the Alberta government over the years to implement Social Credit policies were disallowed by the federal government, struck down by the Supreme Court of Canada, or left unsigned by the lieutenant governor of Alberta.

With Aberhart as premier, the ideological nature of Social Credit was uncertain. On the one hand, the party did emphasize the freedom of the individual over against the power of the state. But on the other hand, it emphasized state action against private financial interests. In the economic sphere, it is not easy to classify early-period Social Credit as being particularly right-wing or left-wing. That would change, however, once Manning became premier.

During his time as leader of the government, Aberhart continued operating his radio ministry, with Manning as his chief assistant. When Aberhart died in 1943, Manning was selected as premier and also took over the radio broadcast.

Manning continued to preach weekly on the program known as Canada's National Back to the Bible Hour during the whole time he was premier. In fact, during this time he managed to expand the program out of its Alberta base into other parts of Canada. Despite his political responsibilities, he would not discontinue national radio evangelism. As biographer Brian Brennan writes, "His mission of leading people toward a personal relationship with God, and turning Canada into a nation of Christian citizens, would continue throughout Manning's premiership and for many years afterwards" (Brennan 2008, 104).

In the 1940s, the Co-operative Commonwealth Federation (CCF) was a new and rapidly growing socialist party in Canada. With Manning as leader, the Alberta Social Credit party became stridently anti-socialist in its efforts to fend off the CCF threat. Indeed, with its monetary theories impossible to implement as policy, opposing socialism became a major theme of the party. Bell writes that "Manning began to see all forms of socialism as equivalent and equally evil" (Bell 2004, 159). The Social Credit party now stood for the "free enterprise way of life" (Bell 2004, 163).

Alberta became a prosperous province as a result of the discovery of oil at Leduc in 1947, and undoubtedly Manning's government benefited from that prosperity. His government was generally frugal and the few minor instances of unethical conduct by members of the government were dealt with quickly and decisively. But the resource royalties enabled the Alberta government to be more generous in its social programs than many other provinces.

In 1967 Manning wrote a book entitled *Political Realignment: A Challenge to Thoughtful Canadians,* in which he argued that the federal Progressive Conservative Party should become more ideologically conservative in order to offer a clear choice for free enterprise voters. Although his ideas were rejected by that party, some observers see them as foreshadowing the Reform Party of Canada, founded by his son, Preston, which did offer a clear ideological alternative to the other major parties.

Brennan recalls that towards the end of his premiership, some people saw Manning as a "dinosaur":

> *It was noted that he still believed in keeping the Christian Sabbath as a day of rest, despite public opinion to the contrary. He alienated young urban voters by refusing to let theatres show movies on Sundays, and absented himself from the legislature when the House approved a measure permitting professional sports to be played on Sundays (Brennan 2008, 162).*

Manning resigned as premier in 1968. He had never lost an election and was still wildly popular among the Alberta electorate. Without him as leader, though, the Social Credit Party was no longer invincible. It continued in power until 1971, when it was defeated by the Progressive Conservatives under Peter Lougheed.

Manning was appointed to the Senate of Canada by Prime Minister Pierre Trudeau in 1970, a surprising move because Manning had been very critical of many key policies of the Trudeau government.

He sat as an Independent Senator until 1983. He continued preaching on Canada's National Back to the Bible Hour until 1989, and died in 1996.

Ernest Manning earned a reputation for running an honest, frugal, and efficient government. It was distinctly conservative. Bell points out that "more than any other government in the country Manning's government embraced, albeit belatedly, the policies of market economics and small government" (Bell 2004, 177). While running the province, Manning was also one of the most prominent evangelical Christian leaders in Canada. His legacy includes distinguished service for both political and religious conservatism, a feat that would be hard to duplicate today.

In short, Ernest Manning is an Alberta legend.

CHAPTER 2

DR. ROBERT THOMPSON OF ALBERTA

During the 1960s, Canada had a national political figure who represented genuine conservatism. Robert Thompson (1914-1997), an MP from Alberta, led the federal Social Credit Party from 1961 to 1967. He had a significant presence on the national political scene for much of the 1960s and was also well-known as an evangelical Christian.

Thompson was born in Duluth, Minnesota in 1914. His father had left Alberta to attend college in Minnesota, married an American girl, and started a family. Having finished college, he took his family back to Alberta in 1918.

Thompson grew up in rural central Alberta, and as a young man came under the influence of Social Credit Premier "Bible Bill" Aberhart. He developed a close relationship with Aberhart and did some organizing for the Social Credit Party. He also trained to be a teacher and then a chiropractor.

In 1940, Thompson joined the Royal Canadian Air Force, and in 1943 was sent to Ethiopia with two other Canadians to help in the East African campaign against the Italians. He remained there for a few years after the war, working in the Ethiopian civil service, and becoming personal friends with the country's emperor, Haile Selassie. In 1951 he left the civil service to work for an evangelical missions agency, Sudan Interior Mission. That came to an end in 1958 when Thompson moved back to Alberta.

In Canada, Thompson once again became involved in Social Credit politics. In February, 1960 he had a public debate with a young Cooperative Commonwealth Federation (CCF) lawyer, Allen Blakeney. Thompson later wrote that the "debate on free enterprise capitalism versus socialism was televised locally, and held in Regina before an audience of more than 1000. The outcome of this debate, while declared a draw by the media, was regarded by many as a victory for free enterprise and Social Credit" (Thompson 1990, 67). Allen Blakeney would later become an NDP premier of Saskatchewan.

Subsequently, Alberta Premier Ernest Manning encouraged Thompson to seek the leadership of the federal Social Credit Party, and gave him the confidence to do so. He became leader in 1961, and was elected in 1962 as the MP for Red Deer, Alberta.

The federal Social Credit Party had 30 MPs elected to the House of Commons in the 1962 election, 24 MPs in the 1963 election, and 5 in the 1965 election. Although the numbers were relatively small, the minority government situation of the Canadian Parliament in the early to mid-1960s gave them some degree of potential influence. As leader of the federal Social Credit Party, Thompson gave speeches across the country outlining his views. As he writes in his memoirs, by 1964 he "was being recognized as a popular spokesman of conservative issues rather than just Social Credit issues" (Thompson 1990, 137).

In 1965 a number of these speeches were compiled as a book entitled *Commonsense for Canadians*, which sold over 40,000 copies. The first speech was directed to those he called "small 'c' conservative Canadians," that is, "all who believe in the importance of the individual in a free society, who are concerned with the inordinate growth of centralized, paternalistic, governmental power." And he points out that at that time, in "Alberta and British Columbia most of these have taken refuge in the Social Credit ranks" (Thompson 1965, 1).

In another speech, where he talks about the distinctive features of Social Credit, Thompson pointed out that "Social Credit is unalterably opposed to fascism, communism and all other forms of socialism which make the individual subservient to the state" (Thompson 1965, 75).

In a speech delivered to the Ontario Sunday School Association, he indicated he hoped Canada would experience an evangelical Christian awakening: "Canada needs a Wesley—urgently so. Canadian Christians desperately need a wave of spiritual revival" (Thompson 1965, 128).

By the late 1960s the federal Social Credit Party was disintegrating in English Canada. The Quebec wing of the party had split off under Réal Caouette. In a controversial move, Thompson decided to run for the Progressive Conservative Party in the 1968 federal election. The PC association in his constituency of Red Deer was not happy about this, but Thompson easily won the PC nomination and then won the seat for the PCs (the same seat he had held for six years as a Social Crediter).

Thompson's switch to the PCs was part of a larger effort. Like Alberta premier Ernest Manning, Thompson thought that if small "c" conservatives in the Social Credit and Progressive Conservative parties worked together, they could form a truly conservative national party. Of course, as we know now, this strategy failed.

By the late 1960s, a new national figure had appeared, Pierre Trudeau. Thompson was not impressed by Trudeau, writing that he came to know him "only after his election as a Member of Parliament, and was immediately critical of his radical left-wing policies" (Thompson 1990, 168).

Thompson served his final term as an MP, 1968-1972, as a Progressive Conservative. In 1972 he became professor of political science at Trinity Western College (later Trinity Western University) in BC, where he subsequently served for a number of years as a teacher and administrator.

In 1979 Thompson wrote a book explaining his personal political philosophy entitled *From the Marketplace: A Christian Voice* in which he lamented the diminishing influence of small "c" conservatism. He stated his conviction that "If the conservative movement is to pick itself up and mobilize its forces so that it can positively contribute to the political scene, then it must bring forth and recognize men of ideas and ideals" (Thompson 1979, 67).

Three years later, Thompson co-authored a book about Canada's constitution with Alberta-born American conservative author Cleon Skousen. Entitled *Canada Can Now Adopt a Model Constitution*, this book points to inadequacies in Trudeau's 1982 constitutional package and advocates a "model constitution" that would restrict the power of government and firmly entrench property rights.

Robert Thompson died in 1997, never having achieved a position in government and therefore never having had an opportunity to implement conservative policies. But he was an important voice for conservative ideas at the national level throughout the 1960s, probably in fact the main spokesman for small "c" conservatism in the federal arena.

He also worked with others in the West to bring the conservative influence of Social Credit activists into the federal Progressive Conservative Party, in an effort to create a truly conservative national party. Despite the ultimate failure of this strategy, it was a noble endeavour that would have paid dividends for the country had it succeeded. Subsequently, he continued teaching and writing, promoting the genuine conservative perspective that is so rare in Canadian political leaders.

CHAPTER 3

PREMIER ROSS THATCHER OF SASKATCHEWAN

One of the most ideologically-minded Canadian conservative leaders in the second half of the twentieth century was a Liberal. Ross Thatcher (1917-1971) was the Premier of Saskatchewan from 1964 to 1971, and he was committed to rescuing Saskatchewan from the socialist principles and policies that had beguiled the province under the Co-operative Commonwealth Federation/New Democratic Party (CCF/NDP) government for 20 years (1944-1964).

Ross Thatcher was born and raised in Saskatchewan. His father was a small businessman who owned some hardware stores; Ross was therefore raised in the family business and learned the importance of hard work and entrepreneurship. As a young man he demonstrated the virtues that would make him a successful businessman, but he soon became interested in politics. In 1942 he was elected to the Moose Jaw city council, and in 1945 he was elected as the Member of Parliament for Moose Jaw in the federal election.

Interestingly, Thatcher was elected as the CCF candidate, that is, as a socialist—for despite his business background, he believed that the CCF offered the best prospect for economic development. During the Great Depression, Thatcher had sympathized deeply with the large numbers of men who wanted to work but were unable to find jobs. For him, providing jobs through economic development had to be the top priority for government. At the time, it didn't matter to him whether economic

19

growth was generated by private industry or government, just as long as the economy was providing jobs.

Because of his business experience and knowledge, Thatcher was somewhat out of place in the CCF caucus. Nevertheless, he survived there because his primary concern was for working people.

Over time, however, he became disgruntled with the CCF's socialist policies. In particular, the provincial CCF government of Saskatchewan had wasted large amounts of money on government-sponsored industries. In 1955, when he was required by the CCF parliamentary caucus to support a policy of increasing corporate taxes, Thatcher left the caucus to sit as an independent MP. Technically, he had been an MP in a socialist party for ten years.

Thatcher eventually joined the Liberal caucus in the House of Commons. He gave a speech outlining the failure of socialism in Saskatchewan. The speech outraged Saskatchewan premier Tommy Douglas (i.e., the CBC's "Greatest Canadian"), who challenged Thatcher to a public debate. On May 20, 1957, the debate took place in Mossbank, Saskatchewan, with Douglas favored to win because of his unrivaled speaking ability. However, Thatcher held his own: most observers concluded that the debate was a draw—but some thought Thatcher had come out ahead. Whatever the case, Thatcher had gone toe-to-toe with Canada's great champion of socialism and was not beaten, a fact that gave him instant credibility.

Thatcher next ran as a Liberal candidate in the 1957 and 1958 federal elections, and lost both times. However, he subsequently became leader of the Saskatchewan Liberal Party in 1959 and began to rebuild it. The Liberal Party was the major alternative to the CCF in Saskatchewan at that time, the provincial Progressive Conservative and Social Credit parties being too small to mount an effective challenge.

Less than a year after becoming Liberal leader, Thatcher faced Tommy Douglas in a provincial election. His Liberal Party made gains, but no one could defeat the legendary Douglas in a Saskatchewan election.

In 1961, however, Douglas resigned as premier to become leader of the federal wing of the CCF's successor party, the New Democratic Party (NDP). Thus in the 1964 provincial election, Thatcher wasn't running against a Saskatchewan legend, and this time Thatcher prevailed while the CCF/NDP socialists lost their first Saskatchewan election in twenty years.

Thatcher's election theme was free enterprise versus socialism. This was now his life's cause. He had seen firsthand what socialism was about, and Saskatchewan had had a socialist government for twenty years with a long trail of socialist policy failures. His speeches contained statements such as, "From hard bitter experience I am opposed to socialism." And referring to Saskatchewan he said, "Canadian socialism was born here. It should be buried here" (Eisler 2004, 249-250).

The fact that Thatcher had been for many years a prominent CCF member in Saskatchewan gave his criticism an especially high level of credibility: he hadn't dropped out of the CCF after just a brief dalliance; he had been hardcore. He could see the realities of economics, and the empirical evidence that mounted over the years was clear: socialism didn't work. Someone needed to rescue Saskatchewan, and Ross Thatcher was the man. As journalist Dale Eisler writes, Thatcher "had migrated politically to become a right-wing ideologue" (Eisler 2004, 250).

He set out to reduce the size of the Saskatchewan government, to make it more efficient, lower taxes, and promote free enterprise. He actively sought investment from US companies to develop the province's natural resources, especially potash and pulp and paper. As he said on the CBC TV program Front Page Challenge, "Our government is cleaning up the rubble left by 20 years of socialism" (Eisler 2004, 260).

During this period, the University of Saskatchewan experienced the same student uprisings as occurred on other North American university campuses. Eisler notes that the "anti-Vietnam war, anti-establishment, anti-U.S. student movement deeply irked Thatcher, who saw it all as woolly-headed socialist thinking" (Eisler 2004, 264).

Thatcher also had his differences with the federal wing of the Liberal Party. He was not a Lester ("Mike") Pearson or Pierre Trudeau kind of Liberal. He saw the NDP as the primary political enemy, whereas the federal Liberals saw the NDP as potential allies. As the emerging Trudeau era would demonstrate, the federal Liberals often favoured socialistic policies. That was not the kind of Liberal Party that Ross Thatcher could support.

Thatcher's antagonism with the federal Liberal Party comes out clearly in Keith Davey's autobiography. Davey was a key campaign director for the party under Mike Pearson. He did not enjoy dealing with Thatcher, whom he accused of taking the provincial party in a "hard right" direction.

The antagonism is apparent from this account by Davey about one of his visits to Saskatchewan:

> *One memorable night I attended a dinner with the Thatch-ers which was addressed by a John Bircher from North Dako-ta, whose extreme right-wing philosophy was more than I could stand. I walked out of the session to be informed later by Peggy Thatcher that I "must have had an unfortunate childhood." And on another occasion, after I had made my presentation to about a thousand delegates at an annual meeting in Saskatoon, Thatcher went to the microphone and said, "Well, you have heard Pearson's man. Is there anyone in this entire room who agrees with anything he has said? If so, will they please stand up." Their knuckles all turned white and Thatcher sneered and said to me, "Well, there it is, Keith. Take that message back to Mike" (Davey 1986, 62).*

During his first term as premier, the Saskatchewan economy grew, unemployment fell, and overall things seemed to go well. In the 1967 provincial election, Thatcher's government was reelected with a few additional MLAs. However, shortly after the election, a recession began in Canada. In keeping with his principles, Thatcher cut government spending because of declining revenues. This move made him unpopular, and he lost the 1971 provincial election to the NDP.

Three weeks later, he died of an apparent heart attack. Just like that, one of Canada's most outstanding champions of free enterprise was gone.

Ross Thatcher should rank high in the pantheon of great Canadian conservatives. He was a Liberal Party premier, but his principles were firmly conservative. Party labels sometimes cause confusion in Canada because the parties often embrace policies at odds with their labels. But there can be no confusion about the political principles and policies of Ross Thatcher: after the socialist period of his youth, he became one of the most genuinely conservative politicians in the latter half of the twentieth century in Canada.

CHAPTER 4

PREMIER STERLING LYON OF MANITOBA

In 1987, notorious NDP MP Svend Robinson described a former Manitoba premier as an "arch enemy of equality." With a recommendation like that, the former premier must have been quite a guy. Indeed, Sterling Lyon (1927-2010), Progressive Conservative premier of Manitoba from 1977 to 1981, was a stalwart small-c conservative who believed in limited government and fought diligently against Pierre Trudeau's proposal for a so-called Charter of Rights and Freedoms.

Sterling Lyon was born in Windsor, Ontario in 1927. Soon after his birth, his mother moved back to her family's homestead at Portage la Prairie, Manitoba. There he grew up and went to school, winning academic awards and earning a reputation for intelligence and intensity.

He subsequently earned a bachelor's degree in political science and history, and then went on to earn a law degree from the University of Manitoba in 1953. He worked as a Crown attorney from 1953 to 1957, and was elected to the Manitoba Legislature as a Progressive Conservative in 1958. Soon he was a cabinet minister in the government of Premier Duff Roblin, and over the years he had charge of a number of different portfolios. Roblin was a Red Tory, and at this stage of his political career, Lyon was comfortable with a larger, activist kind of government.

When Premier Roblin resigned in 1967, Lyon ran for leadership of the Manitoba PC Party but lost to Walter Weir, a genuine small-c conservative. Lyon did not seek reelection in 1969, and afterwards became a corporate lawyer.

He couldn't stay away from politics, however, so he ran for the Progressive Conservative Party in the federal election of 1974, losing to a Liberal cabinet minister. The following year he ran again for leadership of the Manitoba PC Party, and this time won. Importantly, during the early part of the 1970s, Lyon had become more solidly conservative in his political views.

Lyon re-entered the Manitoba Legislature by winning a by-election in November, 1976. Under his leadership, the Manitoba PC Party shifted to the right.

By 1977, the NDP had been in power in Manitoba for eight years. In the provincial election campaign of that year, Lyon declared that his party was a clear alternative to NDP socialism. He accused the NDP of being "the handmaidens of communism." He told a columnist, "My strongest political belief is anti-communism, anti-Marxism, because I think it is the anti-Christ in every sense of the anti-Christ... The only difference between a communist and a socialist [is that] they are both bears, but one has its claws retracted" (Stewart and Wesley 2010, 313).

His three main themes for the election campaign were privatizing crown corporations, reducing the size of the civil service, and cutting taxes. Lyon and his party were easily elected. Political scientists David Stewart and Jared Wesley note that in 1977, "Lyon's Conservatives recorded the highest popular vote total of any single party in the history of Manitoba" (Stewart and Wesley 2010, 316).

Lyon's government reduced corporate and personal tax rates, and tried to reduce government spending, but there was powerful opposition to his program, and a national recession impacted his ability to make positive changes. Thus his efforts to limit government were not very successful. Despite this lack of success, however, Stewart and Wesley argue that "the strength of Lyon's conservative rhetoric and the boldness of his program of restraint define his political career as staunchly conservative" (Stewart and Wesley 2010, 320).

During Lyon's premiership, Prime Minister Pierre Trudeau was making significant changes to Canada's constitution. Among the proposals for constitutional change, Trudeau wanted Canada to adopt a Charter of Rights and Freedoms. Generally speaking, the Charter was essentially intended as a Canadian version of the US Bill of Rights. Trudeau wanted Canada to mimic the American system so that Canadian courts would be able to implement liberal policy decisions, just as the US Supreme Court had been doing in that country since about the 1950s.

More than any other major political leader in Canada at the time, Sterling Lyon saw Trudeau's proposal for what it really was, and he led the fight against the Charter. Lyon pointed out that the Charter was "an alien and unnecessary United States-style innovation that is incompatible with our traditions of parliamentary sovereignty" (Stewart and Wesley 2010, 321). Americanizing the Canadian constitution through the adoption of the Charter would radically change Canada, and it would transfer power from elected politicians to unelected judges. This was the basis of Lyon's opposition. (For more about Lyon's principled resistance to the Charter of Rights, see my book *Leaving God Behind: The Charter of Rights and Canada's Official Rejection of Christianity*).

In the end, Lyon supported the notwithstanding clause in the Charter (Section 33), hoping that it would help to preserve the power of elected representatives in the face of judicial policy-making. In this he would be disappointed.

However, he continued his outspoken support for the clause. In 1986 he wrote in support of its use by Premier Grant Devine's Saskatchewan government:

> *[I]f it had not been for Section 33, there would have been no Charter. It was inserted at the insistence of the eight objecting provinces to ensure that the doctrine of parliamentary supremacy would continue. Any suggestion that its use now is somehow "forbidden fruit" betrays an ignorance not only of its origin, but also of our whole system of parliamentary and responsible government (Lyon 1986b, 57).*

Because of the considerable amount of time he had to spend on the constitutional negotiations, Lyon was distracted from dealing with the particular issues facing Manitoba. When Manitoba held a provincial election in 1981, Lyon was defeated by the NDP, largely because of his unpopular policy of spending restraint; his need to spend time on constitutional affairs, time that might have been spent on the election, however, hadn't helped.

As a result of the election loss, Lyon became the official opposition leader. In this role, he played a key part in slowing the growth of government bilingualism in Manitoba. Popular opinion was strongly behind him on this issue.

Lyon resigned as leader of the Manitoba PC Party in December 1983, and did not seek re-election in 1986. Later that year, he was appointed to the Manitoba Court of Appeal and remained on the court until his mandatory retirement in 2002. He died on December 16, 2010.

Before his appointment to the court, Lyon wrote some columns for *Alberta Report* magazine. In one of these columns he expressed his glowing admiration for US President Ronald Reagan. At the time Reagan was a central hate-object of the Left in Canada, so only a heart-felt conservative would write these words:

> *Ronald Reagan is leading his nation to a much-needed renewal of its spirit of patriotism and common purpose. From the outset of his presidency, he has deliberately and skillfully sought by public statements and policy direction to return America to stability and strength in its economy, national defence and foreign relations. His achievements in reaching these goals are considerable. But more importantly, his ability to distil and articulate the nobler sentiments of his countrymen is helping to rebuild that sense of common values which is the cornerstone of freedom (Lyon 1986a, 45).*

Sterling Lyon should be fondly remembered and emulated by Canadian conservatives. He fought for a vision of limited government and the greatness of Canada's traditional political institutions. Although he wasn't victorious in these fights, he provided an example of political activity based on adherence to principles. He was a genuine patriot and a proponent of conservative Canadian nationalism. Stewart and Wesley state that Lyon's "politics of conviction and his forceful personality made him an icon on the political right." (Stewart and Wesley 2010, 325) He certainly deserves to be an icon for genuine Canadian conservatives.

CHAPTER 5

PREMIER BILL VANDER ZALM OF BRITISH COLUMBIA

One of the best premiers Canada ever had was hounded out of office by means of a fabricated scandal designed to create false impressions about his character. Premier Bill Vander Zalm of British Columbia (1986-1991) was a stellar example of a political leader who genuinely combined social and economic conservatism. He was first known as a provincial cabinet minister for his free enterprise principles. Then as premier, his strong pro-life stance in the wake of the infamous *Morgentaler* Supreme Court decision made him a target of unscrupulous political insiders.

In 2008 Vander Zalm published his autobiography, *Bill Vander Zalm "For the People,"* and the content of this chapter is largely derived from that book.

Bill Vander Zalm was born in the Netherlands in 1934. His family suffered through the German occupation during World War Two, and then immigrated to Canada in 1947. After high school, he got involved in his family's nursery and gardening business. With a strong work ethic and natural business instincts, he was very successful. His family was deeply Roman Catholic.

Vander Zalm was interested in politics and was elected as an alderman for Surrey in 1965.

Despite his conservative principles, he was involved in the federal and provincial Liberal parties. In fact, he was a Liberal candidate in the 1968 federal election, and received the personal support of Prime Minister Pierre Trudeau. Nevertheless, Vander Zalm lost to the incumbent NDP MP.

The following year, however, Vander Zalm easily won election as mayor of Surrey. As mayor, he would be best remembered for the "strawberry picking issue." Basically, in the early 1970s welfare was administered locally by municipalities in BC. Lots of hippies were passing through on their way to Vancouver, and expected to collect welfare in Surrey. As Vander Zalm puts it, "We had no choice but to pay them their so-called 'entitlement,' according to the Federal-Provincial legislation and regulations" (Vander Zalm 2008, 62). This led to financial hardship for Surrey, and threatened to undercut the construction of necessary local infrastructure.

In order to deal with this situation, Vander Zalm developed a common sense proposal. Surrey was an agricultural community in many respects, so his "recommendation was that we would instruct our welfare administrator not to issue any welfare benefits to able bodied, employable people under the age of 45, while there were berries to be picked or potatoes to be dug" (Vander Zalm 2008, 62).

The local Surrey council supported Vander Zalm's solution, and the whole incident received considerable attention, much of it negative. Imagine requiring people to work for a living! What an outrage! Soon afterwards, welfare became primarily a provincial rather than a municipal responsibility.

In 1972 Vander Zalm unsuccessfully ran for leadership of the provincial Liberal Party. Two years later he was recruited by the BC Social Credit Party. He ran as a Social Credit candidate in the 1975 provincial election and won his seat. He was made Minister of Human Resources (which included responsibility for welfare) in the government of Premier Bill Bennett.

Immediately after he was sworn in, reporters wanted to know what his approach would be to government assistance, given his reputation as Mayor of Surrey. Vander Zalm said that the elderly, handicapped and anyone else in genuine need would be treated generously. "But," he added, "if someone is able to work and refuses to do so, they had best pick up a shovel or I'll give them a shovel" (Vander Zalm 2008, 75). The media went ballistic, as did leftists across the province. Some people called this incident the "shovel controversy."

The following week a cabinet meeting was disturbed by a large protest. Premier Bennett decided to allow some of the protestors in to hear what they had to say. As Vander Zalm relates it, "They called for the immediate resignation of Vander Zalm. They shouted, 'Oust the inhumane, uncaring Zalm.' Inhumane because I wanted able bodied people to work instead of collecting welfare" (Vander Zalm 2008, 76).

Vander Zalm was a very effective and successful cabinet minister. Welfare rolls were trimmed as deadbeats and fraudsters were weeded out. "The NDP lambasted me and called me a 'redneck,' to which I replied 'better a redneck than a yellow belly'" (Vander Zalm 2008, 83).

With his no-nonsense conservative approach, Vander Zalm became extremely popular among the grassroots of the Social Credit Party. He was also well-liked by Premier Bennett, and was subsequently given the Municipal Affairs and Transit portfolio, followed by the Education portfolio. The premier saw Vander Zalm as a guy who could fix problems in these ministries.

In 1983 Vander Zalm left politics to go back to running his business. In 1984 he bought a theme park which he named Fantasy Garden World. Later the same year, he ran for mayor of Vancouver but lost to Mike Harcourt. Harcourt would later become leader of the BC NDP and eventually premier of BC.

In May 1986, Bill Bennett resigned as premier, and a campaign for the leadership of the BC Social Credit Party began. Vander Zalm was the twelfth and final candidate to enter the race, and promised that he would bring to government high moral standards based on "true Christian principles." At the leadership convention, he won on the fourth ballot.

He called an election to be held in October 1986. At one Social Credit meeting, a woman stood up and demanded choice for abortion and euthanasia. Vander Zalm replied to her, "I think you're at the wrong meeting. If you really want these things, don't vote for me, vote for the NDP" (Vander Zalm 2008, 228).

Vander Zalm's Social Credit Party won the election with 47 seats to the NDP's 22.

When the BC Ministry of Health produced an inappropriate video on AIDS, Vander Zalm condemned it as the "longest condom ad in B.C. history" (Vander Zalm 2008, 254). He also opposed a school lunch program and a proposal to put condom machines in BC schools. As a result, he was widely condemned for supposedly mixing religion and politics.

But opposition to Vander Zalm really took off after the *Morgentaler* Supreme Court decision in 1988. He announced that the BC government would no longer pay for abortions. He stated, "I want to free taxpayers from the cost of abortions. Abortions diminish society's respect for human life" (Vander Zalm 2008, 282).

In a sense, his courageous and outspoken opposition to abortion would ultimately lead to his downfall. He was constantly hounded about the issue. Even long-time friends and supporters began to avoid him. Protests against his anti-abortion position were held at Fantasy Garden World and began to seriously undermine the business. "Everything, everywhere was about pro-choice, the media newspapers, T.V. and radio talk shows. There was no mention of the baby or the effect of abortions out of control" (Vander Zalm 2008, 287).

The bottom line for his political life was this: "It's true, as has often been said, that this was a turning point in my political career and my popularity as Premier dropped from a very high to a much lower [level]" (Vander Zalm 2008, 325). Even powerful people within the BC Social Credit Party were now working to oust Vander Zalm.

In the summer of 1990, Vander Zalm and his wife Lillian went to a theatre performance of *Les Misérables*. They got more than they bargained for. As he recounts,

> *Some of the crowd clapped, while others booed, when suddenly as we entered the theatre doors we were attacked by a group of militant "gay activists" swinging insulting signs and shoving for all their worth. They spat on both of us and pushed Lillian to the ground. The TV cameras were there to record this scandalous event. Lillian was bruised and hurting, but we still took in the event (Vander Zalm 2008, 389).*

With his popularity declining and their business suffering, Vander Zalm and his wife decided to sell Fantasy Garden World. Unfortunately, they agreed to rely on businesswoman Faye Leung, who caused them much grief and was later exposed in court as a swindler.

With the help of Faye Leung, powerful people in the media and BC politics made the sale of Fantasy Garden World look like some sort of crooked deal on the part of Vander Zalm. With what the public saw as a scandal engulfing his government, Vander Zalm resigned as premier in 1991.

The following year, he was found not guilty by the BC Supreme Court. He was vindicated, but his career had suffered irreparable damage.

A few years later, Vander Zalm attempted a political comeback. He ran as a candidate for the Reform Party of BC in a 1999 by-election, but was unfortunately defeated. Then, from 2009 to 2011, he led a successful campaign to have the Harmonized Sales Tax (HST) repealed in BC.

Canadian conservatives should remember and admire Vander Zalm as a principled and determined fiscal and social conservative political leader. Although his premiership has been clouded by his opponents through their allegations and insinuations, the reality is that Vander Zalm was a very successful cabinet minister and premier.

A number of years ago KPMG, Canada's largest accounting firm, stated, "We can proudly say the Social Credit government, led by Premier Bill Vander Zalm, had the best fiscal and economic record of any government in North America." As well, in 1988 the Dominion Bond Rating Agency said, "British Columbia is the best managed Province in Canada" (Vander Zalm 2008, dust jacket).

It is clear from his long public service that Bill Vander Zalm has been one of the best conservative political leaders in recent Canadian history. Conservatives should not allow his legacy to be determined by his unscrupulous opponents and his leftist adversaries. He deserves to be upheld as a great premier, and someone who was courageous enough to stand for what was right, regardless of the cost to his own career.

CHAPTER 6

PREMIER GRANT DEVINE OF SASKATCHEWAN

Sometimes bad things happen to good people. I would suggest that this helps to explain why Grant Devine (the last Progressive Conservative premier of Saskatchewan) has not received proper recognition as an important conservative leader in Canada. He was sincerely conservative and his government got off to an enthusiastic conservative start, but economic factors beyond his control, and the unethical behaviour of some of his associates, tarnished his legacy.

Grant Devine was born in Regina in 1944 and raised on a farm. After graduating from high school, he went to the University of Saskatchewan, then the University of Alberta, and ultimately earned a PhD in Agricultural Economics from Ohio State University. In 1976 he became a professor of Agricultural Marketing and Consumer Economics at the University of Saskatchewan.

Devine was interested in politics and ran unsuccessfully for the Progressive Conservatives in the 1978 provincial election.

It's important to understand what was happening in Saskatchewan politics at this time. For decades the NDP and Liberal Party were the two main provincial political parties. Under Premier Ross Thatcher (1964-1971), the Liberal Party had really been a conservative party. After Thatcher's death in 1971, it began to lose its conservatism. In 1973, Dick Collver became leader of the Saskatchewan Progressive Conservative Party. Collver was a real conservative, who believed that the socialist government was holding the province back. He said that Saskatchewan was "a sleeping giant…chained by the dogmatic idiots in the NDP" (Baron and Jackson 1991, 11).

Collver worked hard to rebuild the PC Party. In the 1975 election, it went from 0 to 7 seats, and then in the 1978 provincial election it went up to 17 seats, easily replacing the Liberals as the Official Opposition. Nevertheless, Collver resigned as leader in 1979. Grant Devine ran for leadership of the party and won the position in November of that year.

Saskatchewan had been largely dominated by socialist governments since Tommy Douglas became premier in 1944 with his Cooperative Commonwealth Federation (CCF) in 1944. The CCF transformed itself into the New Democratic Party (NDP) in 1961. Except for Ross Thatcher's Liberal government, the CCF/NDP had governed Saskatchewan continuously since World War II.

Before the Great Depression, Saskatchewan had a growing and thriving economy. In 1935 it had the third largest provincial population after Ontario and Quebec. The Depression hit Saskatchewan especially hard, and people turned to the socialist CCF as a way out of economic despair. Unfortunately for the province, the socialist policies of the CCF prevented it from recovering its economic dynamism after World War II. The other western provinces recovered from the Depression, but Saskatchewan never really did. Author Robert Tyre wrote, "Through the booms that saw Alberta and British Columbia move on to breath-taking growth and development, Saskatchewan failed utterly to regain its early sense of growing and building" (Baron and Jackson 1991, 7). That was because Saskatchewan's socialism deterred business growth and investment. The Depression knocked Saskatchewan down, and subsequent socialist policies prevented it from ever getting back on its feet.

Grant Devine understood all this and wanted a better future for his province. He knew that only free enterprise could deliver economic prosperity. Saskatchewan's high taxes and numerous Crown corporations were stifling economic growth. Only by reducing the size of government could individuals and businesses be liberated to achieve their potential in the economy.

University of Regina history professor James Pitsula describes Devine's perspective this way: "He wanted to break the social democratic mold that had been established since World War II and to build a pro-business, entrepreneurial culture. He was of the school of thought that Saskatchewan, if liberated from socialism, could be as prosperous as Alberta. A terrible mistake had been made in choosing the socialist path, but it could be undone" (Pitsula 2004, 318).

In the 1982 provincial election, Devine campaigned on a theme of reducing taxes and promoting growth through free enterprise. He won that election with what Pitsula calls "the largest majority in Saskatchewan political history" (Pitsula 2004, 323).

Immediately, he went to work cutting taxes, the fulfillment of an election promise. He also reduced the government's royalty rate on oil production. As expected, this led to greater development of the oil industry in Saskatchewan. Even though the government's share as a percentage of production was lower, actual royalty revenues increased because of the expansion in production.

Unfortunately, soon the price of oil dropped, which hurt government revenue. As well, grain prices tanked because the US and European Economic Community were aggressively subsidizing their own grain farmers. This put many Saskatchewan farmers in a precarious position and drastically reduced agricultural income. With government revenue dropping as a result of these factors as well as the tax cuts, Saskatchewan began taking on large deficits.

In this depressing situation, Devine's PCs were able to win the 1986 provincial election with a much reduced majority, but had to abandon certain conservative economic policies in order to appeal to the electorate.

Then, with the deficit and debt as serious problems, cutbacks in government spending were essential, which contributed to decreasing popularity for Devine and his government.

In 1987 Devine embarked on a major policy of privatizing Crown corporations. With this policy, Pitsula writes, the "concept of Crown corporations taking a leading role in the economic development of the province was to be replaced by a vision of progress based on individual initiative and private enterprise. It was the death of socialism and Grant Devine was the dragon slayer" (Pitsula 2004, 332). Unfortunately, the success of this program was limited because a sizable proportion of Saskatchewan voters wanted the government to keep the Crown corporations.

To a large degree, Grant Devine's plan to generate prosperity in Saskatchewan through free enterprise was derailed by international economic forces. The province's economy was dependent on agriculture and natural resources (oil, potash, uranium, etc.), and prices for virtually all of these items dropped very low in the mid-to-late 1980s. The NDP easily won the 1991 provincial election, and Devine resigned as PC leader in 1992.

Things got even worse for the PC Party after that. In 1992, large amounts of cash were discovered in some safety deposit boxes. To make a long story short, the cash had been illegally diverted from some PC MLA allowances. After investigation, two PC caucus employees and 12 PC MLAs were convicted of fraud. This incident basically destroyed the Saskatchewan PC Party.

Grant Devine was not involved in the scandal that embroiled many of his fellow PC Party members. But the scandal seriously tarnished the image of his government.

The government of Grant Devine is largely remembered as a period of economic problems followed by scandal. This is really too bad because Grant Devine deserves better.

Pitsula writes that, "At a more fundamental and ideological level, Devine will be remembered for his attempt to steer Saskatchewan away from CCF-NDP 'socialism'" (Pitsula 2004, 349). This is how Devine should be seen by Canadian conservatives. He tried to rescue Saskatchewan from the consequences of its socialist past. Clearly, things didn't turn out as expected, but there can be no doubt that Devine was a genuine conservative and did his best with a difficult situation.

CHAPTER 7

THE CALGARY SCHOOL INTELLECTUALS

In 1998, American political scientist David Rovinsky produced a report showing that Western Canada was becoming increasingly influential in Canadian policymaking. The Reform Party of Canada's dramatic appearance was an important part of that phenomenon, but also important was the emerging influence of a small group of conservative professors at the University of Calgary. Rovinsky termed this group the "Calgary School."

Since that time, the Calgary School has become even more influential, with one of its members, Tom Flanagan, playing a crucial role in the successful career of Stephen Harper. The Calgary School intellectuals punch well above their weight.

There are four key members of the School: Tom Flanagan, Barry Cooper, Ted Morton, and Rainer Knopff. All four are political science professors at the University of Calgary. David Bercuson, a history professor at the same university, has co-written books and articles with Barry Cooper. In this respect he is affiliated with the Calgary School but is not a full-fledged member because he does not share many of the political views of the Calgary School and is a social liberal.

Tom Flanagan began teaching political science at the University of Calgary in 1968. Rainer Knopff joined the faculty in 1978. Barry Cooper and Ted Morton arrived in 1981. Flanagan and Cooper had become friends while graduate students at Duke University in North Carolina in the

1960s. Knopff and Morton had been classmates in the PhD program at the University of Toronto in the 1970s. These four quickly became good friends and shared a generally conservative perspective.

During the 1980s, the men pursued research in their respective fields of expertise, with some publishing books on academic matters. But in the early 1990s, they began producing controversial research that was groundbreaking for Canadian conservatism.

The initial splash occurred in 1991 when Cooper and Bercuson released their book *Deconfederation*, which argued that English-speaking Canada would be better off without Quebec. Three years later, they co-wrote *Derailed*, which called for Canada to return to fiscal responsibility. Cooper later worked for the Fraser Institute while still teaching at the university. He also worked with a group called the Friends of Science to oppose global warming hysteria.

Flanagan became a senior staff member with the Reform Party in 1991 and remained in an official capacity with the party until 1993. He kept in touch with Reform MP Stephen Harper and would subsequently manage his successful Canadian Alliance leadership campaign in 2002, followed by his successful Conservative Party leadership campaign in 2004. Flanagan was also a senior campaign official for the Conservative Party when it won the 2006 election. At the provincial level, Flanagan was the campaign manager for the Wildrose Party in the 2012 Alberta election.

Besides his political activism, Flanagan has produced significant research on First Nations issues, including his award-winning book, *First Nations? Second Thoughts*. He has also written high-profile books on Canadian politics such as *Waiting for the Wave: The Reform Party and the Conservative Movement* and *Harper's Team: Behind the Scenes in the Conservative Rise to Power*.

Like Flanagan, Ted Morton has been active politically. He was elected a Senator-in-Waiting when Alberta held a senate nominee election in 1998. Then he won a seat in the Alberta legislature in 2004 as a Progressive Conservative. He ran for leadership of the Progressive Conservative Party of Alberta in 2006, finishing second on the first ballot, but ultimately losing to Ed Stelmach on the second ballot.

Premier Stelmach appointed Morton to the provincial cabinet, first as Minister of Sustainable Resources and then as Minister of Finance. When Stelmach resigned in 2011, Morton again ran, unsuccessfully, for leadership of the party. Premier Allison Redford appointed him Minister of

Energy, but he lost his seat to a Wildrose candidate in the 2012 provincial election.

Before his intense political activism, Morton had worked closely with Rainer Knopff researching the Charter of Rights. Among the fruit of that research were two key books, *Charter Politics* and *The Charter Revolution & the Court Party*. Morton and Knopff carefully analyzed the leftward drift of judicial decision-making since 1982. Speaking of these two, Flanagan has written, "Rainer and Ted became perhaps the best-known critics of judicial activism in Canada" (Flanagan 2013, 25).

Rainer Knopff has had a smaller public profile than the other members of the Calgary School, probably because his career has followed a more traditional academic path; nevertheless, he was one of the signatories of the famous "Firewall" letter published in the *National Post* in early 2001 calling for Alberta to exercise its constitutional muscle to fend off a threatening Liberal federal government. Among the other signers of the letter were Tom Flanagan, Ted Morton, and Stephen Harper.

Despite the prominence of the Calgary School's members and their influence (both politically and intellectually), it's important to remember that they are a very small group. Flanagan notes that the "Calgary School has never been more than a small part of the department of political science at the University of Calgary; the rarity of conservatives in academic institutions garners extra media attention when a small group of conservatives does get together. It's a man-bites-dog story" (Flanagan 2013, 28).

The Calgary School is outstanding, not because it comprises a large number of intellectuals, but because of the power of its ideas and the superior ability of its members to make an impact either through academic research or direct political activity.

Flanagan writes that "Political movements cannot succeed in the long run without coherent ideas to guide their action. And the Calgary School has been in the forefront, through both academic and popular writings, in developing positions on some of the most controversial issues of the day. They have repeatedly challenged the orthodoxy and political correctness of the left" in a number of important policy areas (Flanagan 2013, 37).

All good things must come to an end, and the Calgary School members are beginning to retire. But they have left a number of "alumni" who are already making an impact on Canadian public life. Among the better known of these are journalist and lawyer Ezra Levant of The Rebel, Danielle Smith, former leader of the Wildrose Party of Alberta, and Ian

Brodie, former Chief of Staff to Prime Minister Stephen Harper and now a University of Calgary professor. Others could also be mentioned. The point is that through these alumni, the Calgary School will continue to pay dividends to the conservative movement in Canada for decades to come.

CHAPTER 8

THE HONOURABLE STOCKWELL DAY

Stockwell Day brought considerable excitement to Canada's conserva-tive movement in 2000 as leader of the Canadian Alliance. Although the excitement did not last, he is still a noteworthy genuine conservative from western Canada.

Stockwell Day grew up mainly in Ontario and Quebec. His father was a federal Social Credit Party activist, so Day was introduced to politics at an early age. His family was close friends with the family of federal Social Credit leader Robert Thompson in the 1960s. Day's father was a man-ager of various Zellers stores, and relatively well-off, although certainly not rich. For a couple of years Day was able to attend a private school in Ontario.

His family moved to BC when Day was in his late teens. He took odd jobs and lived at times like a drifter. In his early twenties he married, and it was through his wife's influence that he eventually converted to evangelical Christianity. He then worked for Teen Challenge, an evangel-ical ministry to teenagers, and later attended a Pentecostal Bible college in Edmonton, ending up as assistant pastor of a Pentecostal church in the town of Bentley, near Red Deer, Alberta. The church had a Christian school, and by the early 1980s the role of private schools in Alberta had become very controversial. Day was by then a leader in an organization of Christian schools, and was therefore quite active in this controversy.

Day had acquired an interest in politics from his parents. In 1982, while assistant pastor at the Bentley church, he tried unsuccessfully to win the PC nomination for the rural provincial constituency he lived in. Four years later, in 1986, he successfully won the PC nomination for a Red Deer constituency. Later that year he was elected to the Legislature.

In his early years as an MLA, Day was known particularly as a defender of the traditional family. The mainstream media was not impressed.

> *Mr. Day's first brush with province-wide prominence came in 1988 when he launched his original public defence of traditional family values. At the time he also argued that homosexuals could be cured of their sexual preference through understanding and counselling. He promptly suffered his first public roasting at the hands of the mainstream press, which has been down on him ever since (Gunter 1992, 37).*

Under Premier Getty, Day was made chairman of the Premier's Council in Support of Alberta Families and chief Tory whip. But he remained on the back benches until December 1992 when the new premier, Ralph Klein, appointed him to the cabinet as Minister of Labour.

Day apparently distinguished himself in cabinet and was made Provincial Treasurer in 1997. As treasurer he implemented a flat tax for Albertans. In 1999 he told "a group of students at McGill University that his 'dream scenario' would be to eliminate provincial income tax within 15 years, preferably with a referendum around the time of the hundredth anniversary of income taxes in Canada" (Hoy 2000, 101). Day was clearly a supporter of limited government and lower taxes.

He resigned as Alberta's Provincial Treasurer in 2000 to pursue leadership of the Canadian Alliance. The Canadian Alliance was formed in January 2000 as a successor to the Reform Party of Canada. The Canadian Alliance was an attempt to unite right-of-centre voters across Canada. Day ran for leadership of the new party and won. He subsequently won a by-election in the Okanagan region of BC in September to get a seat in the House of Commons.

Shortly thereafter, Prime Minister Chretien called a national election for November 27. Chretien's Liberal government easily won re-election and the Canadian Alliance under Day formed the official opposition. Hopes that the Alliance would make a breakthrough in Ontario were disappointed and some party supporters began to blame Day.

Day became increasingly unpopular among his own MPs and in May 2001 some of them left the caucus. In order to bring unity back to the party, Day called for a leadership election. Stephen Harper won the subsequent leadership vote in March 2002. Interestingly, sociologist Trevor Harrison claimed that one of Harper's goals in pursuing the leadership was "to save the party from a take over by social conservatives" (Harrison 2002, 180).

Anyway, Day poured his energy into supporting Stephen Harper as leader and uniting the party. The Canadian Alliance then united with the Progressive Conservative Party of Canada in 2003 to form the new Conservative Party of Canada. When the Conservative Party won the election of 2006, Day was made Minister of Public Safety. He subsequently became Minister of International Trade in 2008 and then president of the Treasury Board in 2010. He did not run for re-election in 2011. Instead, he went back to private life as a business consultant.

Stockwell Day was a well-rounded conservative. He is best known as a Christian social conservative, but he was clearly also a supporter of small government and lower taxes. He would have been a great prime minister.

CHAPTER 9

PREMIER BILL BENNETT OF BC AND HIS GOVERNMENT RESTRAINT PROGRAM

B eginning in 1952 the British Columbia Social Credit Party became the major electoral force in that province for forty years. In 1952 the party unexpectedly won the provincial election, and shortly thereafter selected W. A. C. Bennett (commonly known as "Wacky" Bennett) as its leader. Wacky Bennett served as premier from that time until the party's first electoral defeat to Dave Barrett's NDP in 1972. Basically, the BC Social Credit Party was a moderately right-leaning party that provided the alternative to the CCF/NDP in BC politics.

Wacky Bennett's success was possible because Liberals and Conservatives in BC supported Social Credit in order to prevent a CCF/NDP victory. When many Liberals and Conservatives returned to their own parties in 1972, Bennett lost the election.

Bennett resigned as party leader and MLA in 1973. His son Bill won the by-election to fill his seat and shortly thereafter also became the new leader of the BC Social Credit Party.

According to Bob Plecas, Bill thought it was necessary to move the party to the Left somewhat to win back those who had stopped supporting the party, especially Liberals. Plecas quotes a newspaper report during the 1973 Social Credit leadership race as follows: "Bennett has staked out his position on the left wing, and has made it clear that under his steward-ship there would be a conscious swing toward the ground now occupied by the Liberals" (Plecas 2006, 47). In other words, Bill Bennett was not a conservative.

The Social Credit Party won the provincial election of 1975 and Bill Bennett became premier.

Bill Bennett basically followed the ideological pattern set by his father of a moderately right-leaning or centrist government. His government was re-elected in 1979 and again in 1983. In 1982 he initiated a policy of government cost-cutting because the world recession of the early 1980s was hitting BC hard. However, after the 1983 election, Bennett's government took a more decidedly right-wing shift. It implemented a much stricter fiscal restraint policy, apparently under the influence of the Fraser Institute, a free market think tank based in Vancouver.

The idea of reducing the size and influence of government as a way of dealing with economic problems was an anomaly in Canada at that time. Keynesian economic philosophy ruled the day, and an ever-expanding government was widely assumed to be essential to economic prosperity and growth. Rejection of the Keynesian consensus was considered heresy. Bennett's restraint program thus caused outrage across the country.

What was so outrageous about this policy initiative? University of Victoria political scientist Norman Ruff summarized it this way: "Controls on public sector wages, a cut in the number of public employees, and a reduction in the scope of government activity are the Social Credit solution to the fiscal problems produced by the decline of the British Columbia economy" (Ruff 1984, 153). Simply reducing the size and cost of government was anathema to public sector unions, many intellectuals, and much of the media.

University of Victoria economist John Schofield noted that the "primary goal of the restraint programme introduced by the B.C. government—like that of the Thatcher and Reagan administrations—was to reduce the weight of government in the economy and to stimulate the growth of private enterprise" (Schofield 1984, 41). He then went on to state: "The programme was motivated by the New Right's ideology of anti-collectivism, a fervent hostility toward the state, and a belief in the virtues of rugged individualism" (Schofield 1984, 41). From Schofield's perspective, these were all bad things. But to a conservative or a libertarian, they indicate that Bill Bennett's government was clearly on the right path.

John Malcolmson, at that time a research analyst for the BC Teachers' Federation, viewed the restraint program as being instigated by BC's corporate elite through the Fraser Institute. He wrote:

> *The Institute has had a strong influence on Social Credit policy. Whether it concerns the cuts in social welfare and education, the abolition of rent controls, the undermining of medicare or the assault on public sector bargaining rights, government policy has, in effect, taken its lead from positions staked out by Institute economists and ideologues. The Institute has thus played the role of transmission belt for the social ideas and economic perspectives of the New Right, and as such has played an integral part in the rightward reorientation of Social Credit (Malcolmson 1984, 85).*

In his view, Bill Bennett's Social Credit administration had become "a government of the far right" (Malcolmson 1984, 87).

Plecas writes that Bennett was willing to enact a more severe restraint policy after the 1983 election because he had already decided not to run for reelection himself. The NDP would expend their efforts attacking him, but once he left, the Social Credit Party could select a new leader who didn't carry the opprobrium of the government's policies.

Bennett's 1983 restraint policy was a genuinely conservative initiative. However, Bennett was not really a genuine conservative himself. And he opposed the 1986 leadership candidacy of BC Social Credit's most conservative option, Bill Vander Zalm. Plecas writes that Bennett saw Vander Zalm's leadership as bad for the party: "A Vander Zalm victory was not the outcome he had hoped for. He felt the party was in danger" (Plecas 2006, 267).

So, while the BC Social Credit restraint program deserves notice in a book about genuine western conservatism, Bill Bennett does not himself deserve the title of a genuine conservative.

CHAPTER 10

PREMIER RALPH KLEIN OF ALBERTA
AND HIS GOVERNMENT RESTRAINT PROGRAM

Premier Ralph Klein of Alberta is probably best remembered for his program of government cost-cutting in the mid-1990s. The success of that program was, in fact, a remarkable feat. There are few leaders that can demonstrate an actual decrease in government expenditures. So he does deserve the praise of conservatives for this accomplishment.

However, Klein was not a genuine conservative. This can be seen from his initial political activism as well as policies he would undertake later in his premiership. Some of his first political activism was helping federal Liberal candidates in the 1968 and 1972 elections. As Frank Dabbs notes, "Through the long Liberal drought of the 1970s, Ralph turned up occasionally to assist federal candidates who had become friends, including Nick Taylor, later the leader of the provincial wing of the party" (Dabbs 1997b, 23).

Klein also helped left-wing lawyer Sheldon Chumir win a Calgary seat for the Liberals in the 1986 provincial election. Thus, from the late 1960s through to the mid-1980s, Klein's political sympathies appear to be primarily with the federal and provincial Liberal parties. This does not indicate any preference for conservative views.

Klein was a very popular mayor of Calgary and he was unsuccessfully courted to run as a candidate by the Liberals and federal Progressive Conservative Party. However, Premier Don Getty managed to recruit Klein into the Progressive Conservative Party of Alberta. When Klein won a seat in the provincial election of 1989, he was made Minister of the Environment.

Premier Getty had come to power during a period of low oil prices. As a result, Alberta was suffering economically. Provincial government revenues were low and the province ran a deficit. Getty took the blame for Alberta's poor economic performance and his popularity (along with that of the PC Party) dropped very low. With the Liberals ahead in the polls, Premier Getty announced his resignation in 1992.

There were many candidates for leader of the Alberta PC Party but Klein won on the second ballot. Immediately upon taking office, Klein began to tackle the provincial government's deficit problem. Government spending restraint became his major focus.

The Liberal Party under Lawrence Decore had been leading in the polls for a couple of years or so before the 1993 provincial election. As Dabbs writes, Klein was expected "to pilot the Progressive Conservatives to a stunning but expected defeat" (Dabbs 1997b, 114). Instead, Klein ran an effective campaign that earned the trust of many voters and he won the 1993 election.

Klein's government was serious about spending reductions and government expenditures were, in fact, reduced. This was rather unique, as noted by "Calgary School" political scientist, Barry Cooper in 1996:

> *The significance of the Klein Government's achievement is that they actually put into practice the heretofore merely verbal criticisms of the welfare state. Beginning with the 1993 budget, the Government of Alberta has undertaken to reduce the intrusion of the welfare state in the lives of citizens (Cooper 1996, 10).*

And there was another noteworthy fact as well:

> *Furthermore, the Klein Government meant the phrase "reducing expenditures" in its ordinary sense, namely that they would, actually, reduce expenditures. They did not mean it in its conventionally governmental sense, namely that they would simply spend less than they had been planning to spend (Cooper 1996, 10).*

The results of Klein's efforts were really quite astounding:

> *From 1992 to 1996, Alberta really did experience a fiscal revolution under Premier Ralph Klein. The size of government, as measured by spending on government programs, per person, was*

reduced by 30% in real terms (adjusting for inflation and popula-
tion growth). No other government in Canada, federally or pro-
vincially, has ever reduced the size of government by 30% in real
terms: not Mike Harris in Ontario, not Gordon Campbell in B.C.,
and certainly not Paul Martin in Ottawa (Carpay 2002, 3).

Klein's cost-cutting program received tremendous attention across the country. Reducing the government was for real. Organizations promoting limited government recognized what Klein had accomplished. As political scientist Brooke Jeffrey noted, "In November 1994 he received the Colin M. Brown Freedom Award from the National Citizens' Coalition, and in January 1995 the Fraser Institute presented him with its Fiscal Performance Award—all for his efforts to implement the neo-conservative economic agenda" (Jeffery 1999, 110).

Nevertheless, despite all this fanfare, Klein was not a genuine conservative. He led one of the most conservative policy initiatives in Alberta's history, but this was a matter of circumstance, not conviction.

As a result, once the deficit was under control, Klein reverted to increasing government expenditures once again. John Carpay noted this trend in 2002: "Since 1996, government spending has risen 53%, compared to only 12% population growth and 14% inflation during the same time period. This massive spending increase led to tax increases in the 2002 budget" (Carpay 2002, 3). Many of the benefits of Klein's original spending cuts were gradually lost. Had Klein remained on a fiscally conservative course, the situation would have been very different.

Besides chucking his belief in smaller government, Klein had never accepted social conservatism. This had resulted in conflict at PC Party events where social conservatives pushed for certain policy initiatives.

At the April 1995 party convention, for example, social conservatives proposed a resolution to eliminate government funding for abortion. Klein strongly opposed that proposal.

In a harsh speech, Klein attacked a "conspiracy of the churches" in
his own party for trying to embarrass the party. He said abortion
was a moral question and the legislature was not the forum in
which to debate it. He said he would ignore the will of the con-
vention if it passed the defunding resolution. With all his muscle
out on the floor, however, he was able to beat back the proposal by
only ten votes (Dabbs 1997b, 166).

Klein was not a social conservative and would not support any particular component of the social conservative agenda. Combined with his loss of enthusiasm for spending restraint, it is clear that he was not a genuine conservative.

One other episode of the Klein example is noteworthy. The mainstream media was strongly opposed to Klein's budget-cutting agenda. Despite that, it was the more sympathetic *Alberta Report* that held him to account:

> *Ironically, given the anti-Klein passion of the liberal media, it was the conservative writers and editors of Alberta Report who provided consistent questioning of Klein's policies and legislation. They remained out of reach of his manipulation, challenging him for his failure to extend his conservatism beyond the fiscal arena to include social policy (Dabbs 1997b, 148).*

While Ralph Klein deserves plenty of credit for his reduction in government spending, he cannot be recognized as a genuine conservative. His explicit opposition to social conservatism and his reversion to big government spending policies only a few years after the success of his spending cuts, clearly demonstrate this point.

CHAPTER 11

PRESTON MANNING
AND THE REFORM PARTY OF CANADA

This book is about particular individuals, not political organizations or parties. But it would be impossible to understand Preston Manning without knowing some history about the Reform Party of Canada. The Reform Party was a genuinely conservative party, but Preston Manning cannot be said to be a genuine conservative leader. That is not to slight him. He is a good man who did much throughout his life to make Canada a better country. He is conservative in a sense, but not in the sense of the other leaders described in this book.

After the initial "Trudeaumania" of the late 1960s, much of western Canada had a falling out with Prime Minister Pierre Trudeau. This was most evident in Alberta where every federal seat went to the Progressive Conservative Party from 1972 through 1988.

Trudeau was particularly hated in Alberta after the National Energy Program (NEP) was adopted in 1980. It led to a widespread separatist movement that culminated with the election of a separatist MLA in a 1982 by-election. With the election of a Progressive Conservative government under Prime Minister Brian Mulroney in 1984, westerners (and especially Albertans) thought that their concerns would be taken seriously. However, a large caucus of western Progressive Conservative MPs was surprisingly ineffectual in representing the West's concerns.

Mulroney's government dragged its feet in undoing the policies of the NEP. This upset a lot of Albertans. Others were upset by the general liberal drift of the federal PCs. When the federal government awarded a CF-18 contract to a Montreal firm after a Winnipeg firm had won the bidding for the contract, westerners knew the gig was up. The system was fixed against them.

Many westerners began to wonder if a new federal political party was necessary to bring the West's concerns to the federal government. Ted Byfield, the editor of *Alberta Report* and *Western Report*, began to write columns about such a party and what it would entail. As well, Preston Manning, the son of former Alberta premier Ernest Manning, had been planning for just such an eventuality.

Manning, Byfield, their supporters and other interested people decided to hold a convention of concerned westerners to consider the best alternative for their region. This "Western Assembly," held in April 1987 in Vancouver, voted to create a new western political party. Thus a founding convention for the new party was held in October 1987 in Winnipeg. Most of the activists were from Alberta, but the initial conventions were held outside that province to prevent the new organization from becoming dominated by a single province.

Thus the Reform Party of Canada was born in October 1987. The first leadership contest was easily won by Preston Manning over Stan Roberts of BC.

The Reform Party had candidates in each of the four western provinces (BC, Alberta, Saskatchewan, and Manitoba) for the federal election of November 1988. None of the candidates won, but several in Alberta came second.

After one of the victorious Progressive Conservative candidates in Alberta died, the ensuing 1989 by-election was won by the Reform Party's candidate, Deborah Grey. Later that year Alberta's provincial government held an election to fill a Senate seat. This senatorial election was easily won by the Reform Party's candidate, Stan Waters. In Alberta, at least, the Reform Party was on a roll.

In 1991 the Reform Party decided to become a fully national party that would run candidates in all regions of Canada. Support for the party continued to build during the early 1990s, especially in western Canada and Ontario.

When a federal election was held in October 1993, the Reform Party won 52 seats. One seat was in Ontario and all of the others were in the West.

Because he was the central figure in the creation and success of the Reform Party, it has been widely assumed that Preston Manning is a diehard
conservative ideologue. But this is not the case.

Professor Tom Flanagan, a political scientist at the University of Calgary,
was part of the Reform Party's inner circle in its earliest days and worked
closely with Manning. Flanagan is an ideological conservative and provides an accurate and unassailable assessment of Manning's ideological
disposition. Flanagan is clear that Manning is not a genuine conservative.

In his detailed book about the rise and early success of the Reform Party,
Flanagan points out that "Manning never refers to himself simply as a
conservative; he prefers to say that old distinctions of left and right no
longer apply to the emerging politics of the 21st century" (Flanagan 2009,
10).

He goes on to describe Manning's indifference to modern conservative
thought:

> Manning shows little interest in the revival of conservative think-
> ing in Britain and the United States in the 1980s. Although he
> is an intellectual man who reads widely, he makes no reference
> in his own writings and conversation to leading neo-conserva-
> tive authors such as Friedrich Hayek, Milton Friedman, Thom-
> as Sowell, Irving Kristol, Nathan Glazer, Michael Novak, or the
> public-choice school. Neither in public nor in private does he ever
> refer to Margaret Thatcher or Ronald Reagan as models for what
> he would do if he became prime minister of Canada (Flanagan
> 2009, 11).

Flanagan is not arguing that Manning is a leftist, but that he holds to a
generally more centrist ideological position than consistent conservativism. He goes on to say:

> Of course, Manning holds many opinions that most people would
> call conservative, but they are not supported by an overall conser-
> vative philosophy. He is not consistently and strongly conservative
> in the sense of writers such as William Gairdner, Peter Brimelow,
> and Barbara Amiel, or of organizations such as the National Citi-
> zens' Coalition and the Fraser Institute. Rather, he is eclectic in his
> thinking, and has a tendency to embrace contradictory positions
> in the belief that they will be reconciled in some future synthesis.
> He is certainly not a socialist or even a liberal, but in ideological

terms he could lead a centrist party with a favourable orientation to business (Flanagan 2009, 15).

This perspective influenced Manning's hopes for developing the Reform Party in a less conservative direction. Flanagan writes that Manning envisioned "a dynamic process in which he will recruit centrist or even leftist members, whose presence will change the party's ideological centre of gravity, which in turn will make it more hospitable for centrists and leftists, and so on" (Flanagan 2009, 17).

Manning's ideological inconsistency was noted by some Reform Party members, and it made them uncomfortable. Frank Dabbs writes: "Some of the orthodox right-wing conservatives noticed that Manning was going out of his way to talk about politically neutral populism and reform. 'We are neither left nor right,' Manning frequently said" (Dabbs 1997a, 155). These are not the words of a genuine conservative.

In short, Preston Manning is not a genuine conservative like the men featured in this book. But it was necessary to explain why he is not included. Manning is a great man who did much good for the country. Flanagan is correct in writing that "Manning deserves to be remembered as one of the most influential Canadian politicians who never became prime minister" (Flanagan 2009, 208).

CHAPTER 12

STEPHEN HARPER AND THE PERIL OF POLITICAL COMPROMISE

Some people will likely be surprised and even angry that I have not included former Prime Minister Stephen Harper among the genuine conservative leaders in this book. On the one hand, I can understand that since he was likely the best Prime Minister Canada has had in several decades.

However, to me and many other small-c conservatives, he made too many compromises. I understand that electoral politics requires large scale compromise, and I don't mean any disrespect to Mr. Harper. Without the compromises he made it is unlikely that he could have been prime minister for as long as he was. But those compromises damage his conservative bona fides.

Early in his political career, Stephen Harper was considered to be a principled conservative. After serving one term as a Reform Party MP, he became president of the National Citizens Coalition (NCC) in 1997. The NCC is a conservative organization that promotes limited government and individual freedom. Harper pursued this objective passionately and effectively. However, after leaving the NCC in 2001 to become leader of the Canadian Alliance, Harper began to compromise his conservative principles.

Already in his second year as leader of the Canadian Alliance, he was willing to jettison one of his Christian colleagues for the sake of expediency.

Sacrificing MP Larry Spencer

Larry Spencer was a Baptist pastor who was elected as a Canadian Alliance MP from Regina in the 2000 federal election. He became the party's Family Issues Critic. In 2003 Spencer spoke by phone with reporter Peter O'Neil of the *Vancouver Sun*. O'Neil wrote an article based on this interview that appeared on November 27, 2003. Unfortunately for Spencer, O'Neil inaccurately reported that Spencer had claimed there was a homosexual "conspiracy" and misrepresented Spencer's views on other matters related to homosexuality as well.

Spencer provides a detailed account of these events in his 2006 book *Sacrificed? Truth or Politics*.

O'Neil's article embarrassed the Canadian Alliance leadership and potentially imperiled the merger of the Canadian Alliance and Progressive Conservative parties that was in the works at that time. Stephen Harper immediately fired Spencer from his Family Issues Critic position and Spencer agreed to a temporary resignation from Caucus. He also agreed to issue a public statement of apology written by members of Harper's staff. He writes: "I began to realize that not only had Peter O'Neil laid me on the cross of political death, but that my own party was going to furnish the nails that would keep me there to the last breath" (Spencer 2006, 76).

There was a "media frenzy" over Spencer's alleged comments, but the Canadian Alliance leadership insisted that Spencer avoid talking to the media. He was not allowed to defend himself publicly. Although Spencer had only agreed to a temporary resignation from caucus, there was mounting evidence that the party leadership wanted to keep him out of caucus permanently. As he saw things, "Mr. Harper was quite content to drive in the nails and offer me up as a sacrifice with no further hesitation" (Spencer 2006, 100).

In February 2004 the new Conservative Party caucus voted to keep Spencer out of the party. In the subsequent election of July 2004, Spencer ran as an Independent but was defeated. Stephen Harper had willingly sacrificed a principled Christian man as part of his climb to power.

This was just the beginning. After being elected as prime minister in 2006, Harper would soon begin to disappoint even close friends and colleagues.

Gerry Nicholls of the National Citizens Coalition

One of the people most surprised by Stephen Harper's increasing compromise was Gerry Nicholls, a longtime staff member of the NCC. In his book *Loyal to the Core: Stephen Harper, Me and the NCC*, Nicholls provides an account of Harper's time as NCC president.

Nicholls was completely convinced that Harper was committed to conservative principles. After Harper re-entered electoral politics, Nicholls helped Harper's campaign and was willing to overlook Harper's initial compromises. Eventually, however, Nicholls saw the writing on the wall.

For Nicholls, the straw that broke the camel's back was the Conservative government's March 2007 budget. That budget involved what Nicholls describes as "an orgy of massive government spending" (Nicholls 2009, 150). "After that," Nicholls explains, "I knew Stephen had no intention of providing Canadians with conservative government, or of even paying lip service to conservative ideals. He had turned his back on conservatism" (Nicholls 2009, 151).

Professor Tom Flanagan

That assessment might sound harsh, but it is shared by Tom Flanagan, a political science professor at the University of Calgary. Flanagan was for many years a close companion of Stephen Harper. Flanagan managed Harper's successful leadership campaigns for the Canadian Alliance and new Conservative Party of Canada, and also played key roles in the Conservative Party's 2004 and 2006 federal election campaigns.

After a while, however, Flanagan became concerned about the change in Harper's political direction. Eventually the two men had a falling out. In 2011 Flanagan wrote a letter to the editor of the *Literary Review of Canada* where he described Harper's compromised political perspective as prime minister:

> *Harper has adopted the Liberal shibboleths of bilingualism and multiculturalism. He has no plans to reintroduce capital punishment, criminalize abortion, repeal gay marriage or repeal the Charter. He swears allegiance to the* Canada Health Act. *He has enriched equalization payments for the provinces and pogey for individuals. He has enthusiastically accepted government subsidies to business, while enlarging regional economic expansion. He now advocates Keynesian deficit spending and government bail-*

outs of failing corporations, at least part of the time (Flanagan 2011, 30).

Flanagan, in fact, wrote this letter to reassure certain prominent Liberals that their policies still governed Canada. The "Liberal consensus lives on," Flanagan wrote, "It's just under new management" (Flanagan 2011, 30). Stephen Harper's management.

Betrayed: Stephen Harper's War on Principled Conservatism

More recently another book has been written expressing the disenchantment of some Ontario-based conservatives: *Betrayed: Stephen Harper's War on Principled Conservatism* by Connie Fournier. Connie Fournier is the co-founder (along with her husband Mark) of the Canadian conservative internet forum Free Dominion. The primary goal of Free Dominion is the promotion of principled conservatism.

Beginning in 2001, Connie Fournier became very active in the Canadian Alliance Party, and then the Conservative Party of Canada, at the local level. Free Dominion quickly became popular among Canadian Alliance activists, and when the Alliance held its convention in Edmonton in April 2002, Free Dominion hosted a banquet. A number of Canadian Alliance MPs and National Council members attended. Fournier writes, "Even Stephen Harper, as the brand new leader of the Canadian Alliance, sent us a letter praising Free Dominion for its role in promoting and advancing conservatism in Canada" (Fournier 2015, 24).

After that, however, the Fourniers and other Free Dominion supporters began to fall out with Harper. They considered him to be centralizing too much control of the party in his own hands at the expense of grassroots members. They also thought (correctly) that Harper was trying to marginalize social conservatives within the party, and they opposed Harper's plan to merge the Alliance with the Progressive Conservative Party of Canada.

Connie Fournier wrote her book to convince other conservatives that Stephen Harper has betrayed their movement. She hopes that the Conservative Party of Canada can be restored to conservative principles under a new leader.

Conclusion

In the 2015 federal election, Stephen Harper was clearly preferable to Justin Trudeau of the Liberal Party and Thomas Mulcair of the New Democratic Party. He was the "lesser of evils" among the major party leaders. But that's not a very high recommendation.

In current Canadian politics, conservative principles are often a hindrance to electoral success. The career of Stephen Harper is a clear example of how conservatives can achieve political success by jettisoning their principles to achieve power. But the cost of this kind of "success" is very high. What's the point of attaining power if conservative principles cannot be the guidelines for governing?

"I'd rather be right than be president," said US Senator Henry Clay in 1838. That's an admirable sentiment that Stephen Harper apparently rejected.

PART 2

CHAPTER 13

THE BYFIELD CONSERVATIVE PERSUASION

Note: This chapter was originally written as a standalone article so there may be some repetition with the content of other chapters.

For some Canadians, the meaning of the word conservative can be confusing. This is because there are political parties with that label, namely the Conservative Party of Canada and the provincial Progressive Conservative parties. Unfortunately, parties using the Conservative label often support policies that are not truly conservative.

Normally, political positions described by the word "conservative" revolve around a commitment to principles of limited government and traditional morality. But "Conservative" political parties frequently don't embrace those same principles, and the result is confusion.

Many genuine conservatives in Canada like to refer to themselves as "small-c conservatives" to distinguish themselves from big-C political party Conservatives. This is a good and effective way of making the distinction, but in spoken conversation it can involve a tedious amount of qualification. The fact is that a Conservative may not be a conservative, and a conservative may not be a Conservative.

Sometimes other words are used in combination with the word conservative to clarify a meaning. The term "economic conservative" usually refers to someone who believes in free enterprise, but not necessarily in traditional morality. So we have the phenomenon of people who refer to themselves as economic conservatives and social liberals. Some libertarians can be accurately described this way.

Of course, the term social conservative refers to people committed to traditional morality. In certain cases it also refers to those who oppose gun control and who are skeptical about the policy of mass immigration.

Adding another descriptive term to distinguish one kind of conservatism from another may simply make the situation even more complicated. On the other hand, perhaps the right kind of terminology could help to properly differentiate between different kinds of Canadian conservatives.

I'd like to suggest that there are some conservatives in Canada who can best be labeled "Byfield conservatives." The name *Byfield* comes from the family that founded and operated *Alberta Report* newsmagazine (and its sister publications) from 1973 through to its demise in 2003. Ted Byfield, the patriarch, and his son Link, have had a substantial impact upon western Canada through their writing and publishing over three decades, and they represent a genuine indigenous form of western conservatism demonstrating a firm commitment to at least three basic principles:

1) The vital significance of traditional Christian morality
2) The importance of limited government and free enterprise economics
3) The legitimacy of the political aspirations of western Canada

Each of these three principles can be easily recognized in the writings of the Byfields. In a piece commemorating *Alberta Report*'s twenty-fifth anniversary, Link Byfield wrote about the purpose and identity of the magazine. He stated bluntly that "we are a news medium published by Christians" and that the "first and most fundamental priority has always been the institution of the family" (L. Byfield 1999, 18, 20).

In my book *Standing on Guard for Thee* (Wagner 2007), I identify *Alberta Report* as the single most important print media voice for Christian conservatism in Canada during its 30-year life. As well, I argue that Ted Byfield was one of the three most important spokespersons of Canada's Christian Right during this period (the other two being Rev. Ken Campbell and Gwen Landolt of REAL Women).

The desire for limited government was also apparent in the pages of *Alberta Report*. In an editorial from early 1996, Link wrote about the policies necessary for a free society. He summarized the point this way: "In a free society, the government does only those things which nobody else can: mainly, it passes and enforces laws protecting persons, property and passage." He also lamented that Alberta (and presumably Canada) had become what Hilaire Belloc called a "servile state," namely, "a state which takes ultimate responsibility for everything, reducing its citizens to aimless, irresponsible, petulant servitude" (L. Byfield 1996d, 2).

During the early years of Ralph Klein's premiership, *Alberta Report* championed his efforts to bring the province's finances under control by reducing the size of government.

Besides Christian morality and free enterprise, the interests of western Canada have always been close to the hearts of the Byfields. In the same anniversary article mentioned above, Link pointed out that beginning about 1980, the issue of western political rights "became our defining preoccupation" for about five years (L. Byfield 1999, 19). It was during this period that the magazine reached its zenith as it galvanized western political discontent. After Brian Mulroney was elected in 1984 with a huge contingent of western MPs (including every MP from Alberta), the magazine saw its circulation begin a slow but steady decline.

As I wrote in my book *Alberta: Separatism Then and Now* (Wagner 2009), *Alberta Report* was the single most important media voice supporting Alberta's resistance to Pierre Trudeau's vision of a centralist state. Ted Byfield's editorials articulated an Alberta perspective fiercely at odds with the Trudeau Liberals and their socialistic agenda. Later, he would also take the Mulroney Conservatives to task for their failure to reflect western concerns. Not surprisingly, Ted Byfield and *Alberta Report* played a leading role in the creation of the Reform Party.

The Reform Party was initially designed to run candidates exclusively in western Canada, and the party's first motto was "the West wants in." Many conservatives in western Canada felt that their region was being ignored in national affairs and they needed a new political vehicle to carry their concerns to Ottawa. As well, socially conservative westerners and free enterprising businessmen wanted a vehicle to counter the liberal social bent and penchant for spending of Mulroney's Progressive Conservatives.

As the Reform Party expanded into eastern Canada, it dropped its western focus and much of its social conservative spirit, although it continued to advocate limiting government. But the distinctive traits of Byfield conservatism could later be discerned in the political movement supporting former Alberta cabinet minister Dr. Ted Morton's candidacy for leadership of the provincial Progressive Conservative Party. As well, it may be that the Wildrose Party has become the current organizational home of this same political movement. Link Byfield, in fact, has been a central figure in the Wildrose Party from its inception.

The bottom line is that there is a distinctively western Canadian brand of genuine conservatism that continues to embrace elements of social conservatism as well as western regional aspirations. These elements differentiate it from some other forms of conservatism in Canada. Perhaps the phrase "Byfield conservative" could be helpful for distinguishing this particular branch of Canada's conservative movement.

Postscript: After this article appeared on the Freedom Press Journal website, Link sent me an email (August 16, 2013) stating: "Thanks for writing this – I don't know quite what to say, or what should be said, except that we are both honored and appreciative. Whether your thesis is sound I must leave to others to decide – but I very much enjoyed considering it."

CHAPTER 14

THE POWERFUL INFLUENCE OF *ALBERTA REPORT* MAGAZINE

The most important media voice western Canadian conservatism ever had was *Alberta Report* magazine and its associated publications. In the early 1990s, one conservative activist told me he considered *Alberta Report* to be the "political Bible" of southern Alberta. It was loved and taken seriously by tens of thousands of westerners.

It would be impossible to precisely measure the influence of this magazine, or any print publication for that matter. Nevertheless there is plenty of evidence to suggest that its influence was significant and meaningful.

Early in 2008, the magazine trade journal *Masthead* published the results of a reader poll under the heading, "Canada's 20 Most Influential Magazines of All Time." *Alberta Report* was ranked 13th out of 20. *Masthead* wrote the following about the magazine:

> *A lot of people hated* Alberta Report. *They called it homophobic, sexist and racist; Western ideological madness at its very worst. A lot of people loved* Alberta Report. *They called it honest, fearless and engaging; a lone voice for Christian conservatives in a country ruled by atheist liberals. Ken Whyte once called founder and owner Ted Byfield "a right-wing redneck radical." A lot of journalists have said similar things. Ken Whyte has also called* Alberta Report *the best place he ever worked. A lot of journalists have said that, too.* Alberta Report *may have died in 2003, but echoes of its loud, brash voice can still be heard today in blogs, in the back*

*pages of newspapers, in Edmonton, in Calgary, in Ottawa. "At
the time, it was considered to be very marginal," left-wing activist
Judy Rebick once said. "It turned out later to be basically in the
vanguard of elite conservative thought" (Alberta Views 2008, 19).*

Other critics have also noted the influence of the magazine. Writing in
1995, sociologist Trevor Harrison pointed out that "*Alberta Report* has
been, since its inception, western Canada's most prominent and consistent organ for the dissemination of conservative values" (Harrison 1995,
51). He also noted the circulation figures for the magazine in its three
forms: "In June 1991 *BC Report* had a paid circulation of 21,000, *Alberta
Report* approximately 40,000, and *Western Report* about 1500" (Harrison
1995, 51).

Premier Peter Lougheed on the influence of *Alberta Report*

No less a person than former Alberta premier Peter Lougheed wrote an
appreciation of *Alberta Report* on the occasion of the magazine's twenty-fifth anniversary. He clearly indicated that *Alberta Report* was an influential publication. In particular, it played an important role during the
conflict between the province and the Trudeau government over Alberta's oil and gas resources.

At that time of crisis, Lougheed explains, "*Alberta Report* was fully sup-
portive of Alberta's position and very effective in helping to communicate
the Alberta point of view" (Lougheed 1999, 12).

The Alberta government had no choice but to fight back against Pierre
Trudeau's National Energy Program (NEP). The magazine explained why
the fight was necessary. "Week after week the *Alberta Report* made it clear
to Albertans, and also to Canadians, that the federal government was
attempting to destroy the right of ownership of oil and gas by Albertans"
(Lougheed 1999, 12). This was noticed by the federal government, for as
Lougheed wrote, "we discovered many Ottawa politicians, bureaucrats
and journalists at the time were reading the magazine intensely, and col-
lectively coming to the conclusion that Albertans were united in taking
such a strong stand against this attack upon their resources" (Lougheed
1999, 12).

Nevertheless, *Alberta Report* was not a cheerleader for the Lougheed government. The magazine was frequently critical of various provincial policies. However, as the former premier wrote, "on the major national issues

involving Alberta, as I have described, the support by the *Alberta Report* was strong and its impact was very significant and positive" (Lougheed 1999, 12).

Prairie Report

The Canadian Broadcasting Corporation (CBC) could not ignore *Alberta Report* and it eventually produced a play written by one of the magazine's former employees, Frank Moher.

Frank Moher was the book review editor of *Alberta Report* from 1983 to 1986. When he began working for the magazine he did not have any developed political views, although he appreciated its pro-Western perspective. Over time, however, he developed fashionably left-wing views and began to resent *Alberta Report*'s conservative perspective.

After leaving the magazine and moving to BC, Moher wrote a fictional play called *Prairie Report* based on *Alberta Report*'s editorial room. The Ted Byfield figure was named Dick Bennington and Ted's son Link was named Otis Bennington. The main storyline involves the takeover of *Prairie Report* magazine by an eastern businessman who wants to change its pro-Western editorial direction.

In his introduction to the play, Moher pays tribute to the influence of Ted Byfield through the magazine. He writes that "Ted has harvested his bounty; he has managed to accumulate enough power over the years to begin reshaping the political agenda, at least in Alberta, and to use his ubiquitous identification with all things western to place his very profile upon the land" (Moher 1990, 19). In Moher's view it is clear that *Alberta Report* has influenced the province's politics to a large degree.

He doesn't think that influence has been good, however. In one section of the play he seems to blame it for gay bashing in Edmonton. One of the fictional magazine's writers is Pauline Brett, a left-wing feminist who nevertheless works for the magazine (a fictional Paula Simons). At one point she says to Dick Bennington: "You write your columns about homosexuals, careful to condemn the sin but not the sinner, of course. And then some nut uses them as an excuse to go down to the strip and beat up a few gays" (Moher 1990, 86). The implication of these sorts of false allegations, of course, is that banning any expression of opposition to homosexuality is the solution to violence against gays.

As mentioned, Moher's play was subsequently produced by the CBC. Apparently the CBC had been paying attention to Ted Byfield for a few years, as he explained:

> *One of the penalties you pay as proprietor of the last domestically owned general news publication in western Canada is the necessity of being recurrently "explained" by the CBC. Twice in the last couple of years I have been featured on CBC programs. I was the subject of a half-hour television documentary (dangerous ideologue) and a lengthy "treatment" on the national radio show,* Sunday Morning *(religious fanatic). Now I notice that the CBC is prominent among the sponsors, and plans a national review on television, of yet another explanation, this one a stage play about this magazine called* Prairie Report *where I am once again featured (peevishly pompous bore) (Byfield 1988e, 52).*

Byfield saw the play performed at the Kaasa Theatre in Edmonton and then wrote a column about it in *Alberta Report*. After discussing the play itself, he moves on to address the issue of a distinctively western Canadian identity within the arts. This is apparently what Frank Moher would like to develop. But Byfield argued that setting out to achieve that goal would be a waste of Moher's talent:

> *Because the first rule of any kind of creativity is, surely, that you do not achieve originality by striving for originality, and you cannot become unique by trying to be unique. If our western playwrights, artists, composers, and, heaven help us, publishers, want to accomplish a western Canadian school of anything, then the very first thing we must do is forget about being western Canadians. There are a thousand dilemmas and problems facing humanity in the late 20th century that have never faced us before. They are as pressing in Paris as they are in Pincher Creek, and if we have things to say about them, then we should say them, not in order to establish our uniqueness, but because we think they should be heard. And if they are valid and well stated, then we shall certainly discover ourselves to have been unique, though that had been the farthest thing from our minds (Byfield 1988e, 52).*

Ted Byfield demonstrated this very point with his own work. By addressing the issues facing western Canada from his decidedly Christian perspective, he developed the form of conservativism that can accurately be called "Byfield conservatism."

Alberta Report's Coverage of Homosexual Rights Matters in the 1990s

Alberta Report was perhaps most controversial in its coverage of homosexual rights. The cause of homosexual rights began to gather momentum by the late 1970s and was advancing rapidly by the 1990s. The magazine's coverage of this issue increased accordingly.

Feminist researcher Gloria Filax conducted a detailed analysis of *Alberta Report*'s coverage of homosexual issues from 1992 to 1998. Homosexual rights issues loomed large during that period and numerous articles, including cover stories, appeared in the magazine on that theme. Interestingly, Filax conducted her analysis because of *Alberta Report*'s perceived influence over Alberta's leaders and populace. As she put it, "While in many ways a fiscally marginal magazine, *Alberta Report* had a significant impact on discourses about social values" (Filax 2006, xiii).

Interestingly, Filax also acknowledges that the magazine paid attention to homosexual rights issues in a way that other media outlets did not:

> As well as being a ubiquitous presence in Alberta, remarkably, Alberta Report had the most complete and comprehensive coverage of queer issues in the province during the 1990s. Unlike the mainstream media, Alberta Report took (the perceived threat of) sexual minority peoples seriously (Filax 2006, xiii).

In some sense this could be seen as a backhanded compliment. But the main point of this information is to register another knowledgeable observer attributing noteworthy influence to *Alberta Report*. It is clear that many of the magazine's critics considered it to be an important factor in Alberta society. People from across the political spectrum could agree on this point.

CHAPTER 15

THE POLITICAL THOUGHT OF LINK BYFIELD

Link Byfield was taken from us too soon. When he passed away in January 2015 it seemed like the heart was cut out of Alberta conservatism. There is a void that no one else can fill.

Unfortunately, Link did not write a book explaining his perspective on social and political matters. On the other hand, he left hundreds of columns and articles that serve the same purpose. Although they are written about events that were occurring at a particular time, they often contained expressions of social and political philosophy that transcend those past events. They have an enduring significance that are still worth considering.

Limited government

One leg of the Byfield conservative perspective is the belief in small, limited government. To a certain degree this perspective reflects a kind libertarianism. Government should do only what cannot be done by individuals or intermediary groups (such as families, churches, community organizations, etc.). Having a small government means that taxes are low and the economy can prosper as entrepreneurs develop businesses and workers keep the money they earn.

In the early 1990s provincial governments, as well as the federal government, were spending way beyond their means. Deficits were the norm and government debt was growing astronomically. Link Byfield was a leader in speaking out against such largess. "It is just plain wrong," he wrote, "to tax future generations for things that government and its massive fiefdom of interest groups are needlessly consuming today" (L. Byfield 1992, 2).

Link realized that regular citizens were often at fault for the government we had. In some respects Canadians had changed for the worse since about the 1970s:

> We long ago ceased to be a very principled population. It was we who allowed the present elites to go on a spending spree with the accumulated moral and financial capital of the nation, and once something is gone it is gone. People are now very comfortable deciding how disproportionate a tax their richer neighbours will pay; with "experts" dictating how we will raise our children and which amoral doctrines will be taught in our schools; with government knowing every last detail of our personal lives, political activities and finances. So long have we cocooned ourselves in this democratic totalitarianism, most of us can scarcely imagine any other existence.
>
> A truly free democracy builds up other institutions independent of government or it becomes nothing more than a roving mob looking for loot. First and foremost, it does not intrude into family life and the raising and teaching of children. It gives to the family a small institutional sovereignty all its own. Secondly, it honours religious institutions which teach about God and right and wrong. These do not exist for civic purposes, and in some ways they are indeed "intolerant." But they alone serve as a bulwark against the baser instincts of man, especially envy, which is blood poison in a free state (L. Byfield 1992, 2).

Although the diagnosis was grim, there was still hope. Canada could once again become a "truly free democracy." Link put it this way: "Canada was once such a democracy, and it can be again. But whether it will find the necessary courage and intelligence to save itself depends, if you think about it, upon you" (L. Byfield 1992, 2).

Link was calling upon his readers to take the steps necessary to right the country. And this is still the way forward. Change starts with us as individuals. First we change ourselves, then we can change the country. Improving the situation begins with you and me.

When the government of Premier Ralph Klein embarked on a major effort to reduce government spending in the early to mid-1990s, Link applauded loudly. Under Klein, yearly expenditures by Alberta's government did, in fact, shrink. The effect on the provincial economy was positive. As Link put it, "while Alberta's government has been shrinking its private sector has been growing very steadily. This is good, because the private economy is also the voluntary economy—the carrot economy. Governments compel. Markets persuade" (L. Byfield 1996b, 2).

This again reminds us of the proper role of government: "A wise state remains small and restricts itself to doing those things which it alone can do—things like protecting us from criminals and collecting taxes" (L. Byfield 1996b, 2).

Interestingly, Link returned to this theme again in early 1996 and provided an extended explanation of his view:

> In a free society, the government does only those things which nobody else can: mainly, it passes and enforces laws protecting persons, property and passage. It does not dispense pills, it does not tell parents where to send their children to school, it does not distribute sandwiches to the lazy and the destitute, and it does not force people, except in the most dire emergencies, to pay taxes for things they find morally vile.
>
> Now you will notice that government here does all of the above. It runs all the hospitals and pays all the doctors. It is beginning to decide what sort of children it can afford and which ones it wants killed before anyone becomes too attached to them. It decides where children will go to school, who will teach them, what they will learn and what attitudes they will absorb. It runs a plethora of welfare and social intervention programs, it refuses to enforce marriage vows, and it indirectly subsidizes divorce, absentee parenting and youthful defiance. It forces families to fund things through taxes they find utterly repugnant—particularly the killing of prenatal children.
>
> In short, we have what historian Hilaire Belloc called the modern "servile state"—by which he meant a state which takes ultimate responsibility for everything, reducing its citizens to aimless, irresponsible, petulant servitude (L. Byfield 1996d, 2).

Bullying

When government is confined to its proper role, citizens must step up to fulfill their own responsibilities. One example where this can and should be done involves bullying.

Bullying in schools is one of the politically correct issues that is currently very trendy in Alberta and across the country. All the fashionable people are condemning bullying in schools and calling for more and tougher laws against it, especially if the victim is homosexual or transgender. Despite the fact that bullying has been happening in schools for generations, it is now seemingly the cause du jour.

Link, however, had addressed this issue almost twenty years beforehand. Towards the end of 1995 a 13-year-old girl named Jamie Topott was being regularly bullied in her junior high school, G. M. Egbert Community School. The situation became so serious that nine students were charged by police for offenses related to Jamie's victimization.

Link used this situation to call upon parents to take their responsibilities seriously, and to point out the consequences of the parents neglecting their responsibilities. Schools are supposed to be an extension of the home and parents' authority, but our society has lost sight of this concept. It has become widely held that schools are the prerogative of the state. What this has done, wrote Link,

> is nurture a monster that isn't subject to the authority of anyone. Not of parents, because they have been deliberately denied any decisive role for two or three generations. Not of the school staff, because they by themselves have no authority. And not of the state, because the state doesn't know the children, nor can it determine the best interests of any of them, however much it may like to pretend otherwise (L. Byfield 1996a, 2).

That being the case, the responsibility for the situation returns to the parents. The parents of the children attending the school must take action to address the bullying and stop it. Link states plainly, "The people at fault for Jamie's plight are the parents of that school. If there is bullying, what are they doing about it? If they are trying to restore order, and the staff or the local bureaucracy are preventing them, then what are they doing about that?" (L. Byfield 1996a, 2).

It all comes down to the parents and their taking responsibility for their children and their children's education:

> G.M. Egbert is an extension of their homes. If they are sending their own children to a juvenile prison run by the inmates, it is

their business to get it back on track. If they wait for the govern-
ment, or the board, or the staff, or the police to do the job for them,
they will wait in vain. It won't happen (L. Byfield 1996a, 2).

Indeed. And this is the conservative solution to bullying in schools: parents taking their responsibility seriously. But current debates over bullying
seem to have left parents out of the picture and focused on heavy-handed
legislative solutions.

The key point, though, is that in a society with a small, limited government, citizens need to take responsibility seriously. People who constantly look to the government for solutions to every problem will end up with
a large, bloated government that consumes an ever-increasing percentage
of the national wealth and begins to squeeze out individual liberty. A
free society cannot last when the populace wants the government to "do
something" about every problem they encounter. Freedom requires responsibility, and school bullying can be addressed by parents rather than
relying, once again, on the government.

Social conservatism or theo-conservatism

It will surprise no one familiar with the Byfields and their publications
that Link was a strong advocate for social conservatism. Others have referred to this perspective as moral conservatism or theo-conservatism.
These terms are all perfectly suitable.

In 1988, before the Reform Party of Canada had really taken off, Link
wrote a favourable column about the Christian Heritage Party of Canada
(CHP). In describing the CHP's perspective, Link reveals his sympathy
with theo-conservativism:

The CHP's central thesis is that law and government have always
been based on systems of morality, and that Canada's, like Brit-
ain's, rest specifically on Christian morality. To the extent these
precepts have been cast aside in the last few decades we have, as a
direct consequence, suffered.

It's a convincing argument. If you deliberately destroy moral con-
sensus, you are soon left without legal and economic consensus.
Private vice and amorality follow in due course, and lead swiftly
and directly to public vice and amorality (L. Byfield 1988, 4).

Link then describes how this has played out in Canada:

Parliament decriminalizes sodomy, and sodomists promptly (and with perfect logic) demand the right to marry one another and adopt children. It legalizes pornography, and pornographers (sensibly enough) demand the right to sell even their most lurid products in neighbourhood grocery stores. It deliberately removes the stigma of legal or social guilt from those who are lazy, unfaithful, greedy or crooked, and these people then presume they are virtuous. Whether we like it or not, laws serve as a reflection of what the public believes to be right and wrong. If a practice isn't illegal, it is by implication acceptable (L. Byfield 1988, 4).

Link never wavered in his commitment to the historic Christian perspective on sexual morality. This, of course, was reflected in his outspoken opposition to homosexuality. He believed that legalizing homosexuality had been a mistake. Referring to the homosexual rights movement he wrote:

Throughout North America their social and political influence has gained remarkably in strength and evil. This is not surprising in a society which 20 or 30 years ago lost its understanding of the reality of right and wrong, virtue and sin. And it is not surprising that sodomites, who best reflect that loss of understanding, are its most pathetic, most unrepentant and most unhappy victims. Let us not hate them. They are too wretched for that. But at the same time, we must restore all the legal and social prohibitions against unnatural sex we have so liberally pitched out since (L. Byfield 1990, 4).

Freedom as "self-government"

In February 1996, Patrick J. Buchanan won the New Hampshire primary in his campaign to become the Republican Party presidential candidate in the United States. That event set off an avalanche of criticism against Buchanan who the mainstream media condemned as a right-wing extremist. Link, however, wrote a column in defence of Buchanan and used it to explain some aspects of conservative thought.

Link wrote that Buchanan's positions were not weird or extreme at all. Buchanan simply held to "the old populist conception of government, that the role of the state is to protect individuals, families and communities in the free exercise of their God-given responsibilities" (L. Byfield 1996c, 2).

Buchanan, Link wrote, "is a true conservative, who recognizes an unbreakable connection between rights and responsibilities, and that private choices have public consequences. And he is a Christian, who believes that liberty comes from God" (L. Byfield 1996c, 2).

At this point Link provides a brief description of how the meaning of the word "freedom" has changed since the 1960s. Freedom now means doing what we want rather than doing what we should. He explains the older conservative view this way:

> A synonym for freedom is "self-government." If we are self-governed, we can say we are free. It means that we have control over ourselves. And it also means that if we have lost control over ourselves, we have lost our freedom. We descend either to a state of slavery or to a state of anarchy; in our case, the latter (L. Byfield 1996c, 2).

The idea of freedom as "self-government" is important for understanding the difference between classical and modern conceptions of freedom.

Take, for example, the case of a man who is in a position to view pornography without anyone finding out. He is strongly tempted and is faced with the choice of giving in to the temptation, or turning away from it. In the modern view, true freedom means doing what he really desires, so he views the pornography. This is what he feels he wants, so he does it. He is "free" to fulfill his base desires.

In the classical view, however, true freedom means he forces himself to turn away from the pornography and ignore it. How can this be called "freedom"? Because his mind overrules his passions so that he could do what is right. He is in control of himself rather than being controlled by biological urges.

When a man gives in to his physical desires he is not free, he is controlled by his physical desires. Every animal gives in to its desires, so in following this path the man who views the pornography is actually a slave to his animal desires. He is controlled by his passions and therefore cannot be considered "free."

The other fellow, the one who turned away from the pornography, is in an entirely different situation. He exercised self-control or self-government. He governed himself, rather than allowing bodily appetites to govern his behavior. He is truly free because he consciously made himself do what is right instead of giving in to his desires. It is this self-controlled kind of individual that is required for limited government to succeed because he has internal controls of self-discipline rather than needing external controls of government compulsion.

The more that citizens exercise self-restraint and self-control, the less government that is needed. A society with a small and limited government can only exist for the long-term when the population has this kind of virtuous character.

Frustration with the Supreme Court

The leftist orientation of the post-1982 Supreme Court of Canada provided much fodder for conservative criticism. The outcome of many cases dealing with political or social policies could easily be predicted beforehand since the leftwing slant of the final decision was rarely in doubt.

In a 1997 ruling, the Supreme Court struck down a Manitoba government requirement that a pregnant, drug-using mother receive treatment for her drug use to protect her unborn child. The court refused to recognize the unborn child as a person with rights. Around the same time, the court also heard the appeal of Delwin Vriend who wanted to compel the Alberta government to include sexual orientation in its human rights legislation. According to Link (and he would be proven right), the court had made it plain during the appeal hearing that it would rule in Vriend's favour. Link described the situation this way:

> The baby in the way of its mother gets killed. The homosexual with his multiple enthusiasms is left free to spread the intestinal parasites and venereal diseases for which he is medically famous, and not only may he not be punished, he may not even be admonished (L. Byfield 1997, 2).

In 1996 *Alberta Report* published an essay by a Calgary medical doctor, Gisela Macphail, which explained some of the medical consequences of homosexual behaviour. The essay was based on a presentation Dr. Macphail had made to the Calgary Board of Education. She wanted the health effects of homosexual behaviour to be taught in schools so that students could make wise sexual choices.

Dr. Macphail was a specialist in infectious diseases and had treated many homosexual patients. She was not a "homophobe," but a caring physician who believed that people should make informed decisions. To make good decisions people need accurate information. Withholding such information does not help them, it hurts them.

Much of her essay is an explanation of the kinds of diseases spread by various homosexual acts. For example, she wrote: "Any practice which facilitates direct or indirect oral-rectal contact will enable the spread of fecal and rectal micro-organisms to the sexual partner" (Macphail 1996, 33). Among the various health effects of these sorts of activities, "passive anal intercourse carries a 30-fold increased risk of anal cancer compared to controls" (Macphail 1996, 33).

Much of the material contained in Dr. Macphail's essay is simply gross. That's because homosexual sexual activity is gross and she had to explain how it affects health. She noted that about 83 percent of HIV cases in Alberta are in men who had sex with other men, and she concludes as follows:

> I only want to say that behaviour is a choice. It can be modified. Students seeking counselling with respect to their sexuality need information about possible health effects. They need to know the consequences of their choices and about alternatives such as postponing sexual involvement and non-sexual expressions of intimacy (Macphail 1996, 33).

The information presented by Dr. Macphail clearly supports what Link had written about health problems associated with homosexuality.

The *Vriend* decision was released by the Supreme Court in April 1998. This decision added sexual orientation to Alberta's human rights legislation despite the Alberta legislature's conscious decision not to include it. There was considerable anger in parts of the province as a result. Many Albertans did not appreciate a federal court writing provincial legislation. Link articulated this point clearly:

> Other Canadians imagine that Albertans get angry about gay rights because we hate gays. This is not true. We couldn't be bothered hating gays. We get angry because we don't like—and don't accept—being told by outsiders how we will live, what we will think, and what our provincial laws will say. And this goes double when the people doing the telling are a panel of fat-headed, over-paid Ottawa lawyers in red suits who alter our laws at a whim and answer to no one. Our laws do not belong to these Ottawa lawyers, whose stupidity about charter rights grows more wanton and reckless by the year. Our laws belong to us (L. Byfield 1998, 2).

Christianity versus Secular Humanism

For the twenty-fifth anniversary edition of *Alberta Report*, Link wrote an essay on the magazine's past and he also sketched out a path for its future. Among other things, he discussed the two main worldviews struggling for control of Canada (and the other countries of the Western world). One was the Judeo-Christian worldview upheld by *Alberta Report*. The other was the secular humanist worldview that dominates government and the mainstream media.

Many people who do not consciously hold to a particular religion think that they do not have any form of religion. But they do. They are just unaware of it. Secular humanism is the religion that claims to be the absence of religion. It is a new religion that many people hold by default. Link described it this way:

> *Many people who see the world through eyes unenlightened by faith in some form of Judeo-Christian creed come to conclude that human life is governed by impersonal forces. There is the force of nature, the force of economics, the force of government and the force of death. Ultimately, all that ties the individual to his family, employer and society is his own self-interest in minimizing larger, random hazards. The individual is everything. He creates by choice his own moral and spiritual universe. The self is ultimately what life is all about. Such is the new religion. If you doubt this, go read the lifestyle headlines at the nearest magazine rack (L. Byfield 1999, 20).*

According to Link, this line of thought began in Europe over 300 years ago. It's a common way of thinking that for most of its adherents has no name at all.

> *Nonetheless, this new faith informed the oft-cited Humanist Manifestos of 1933 and 1973, both of which explicitly identify it as a religion. It is now the accepted faith of the governing class, and unofficially that of society. It pervades academe, public administration, commerce, education, law and the news and entertainment media. Christianity is tolerated only if it submits to the new orthodoxy; at which point it ceases to be Christian.*

> *Those of us who still assert the older faith can clearly see the ruin and misery the new religion of the self has brought with it: divorce, high taxes, rampant crime, and a spreading sense of lost honour and alienation (L. Byfield 1999, 21).*

The new religion has been extending its control over the various institutions of society and this did not bode well for the future of political liberty and the religion which gave birth to liberty, namely Christianity. We don't know what the political outcome will be.

> But one thing above all else is obvious: the family, more than any other institution, is what the new religion must destroy. The schools it captured long ago, and the media. The social authority of the church is gone, having been reduced mainly to Catholic bishops and Protestant moderators uttering socialist irrelevancies. But the family, though badly weakened, remains in place. And as long as it remains, the new religion is not secure.

> It is not secure because the family, as G.K. Chesterton pointed out most of a century ago, represents a mini-sovereignty. Left in peace it soon becomes a little republic, a small self-governing common-wealth. It can adopt beliefs, set rules, form opinions, teach its children, visit its neighbours, build a church and form a culture—all without help or permission from the state. And until this century, throughout all of history, this is exactly what it did.

> All of these activities are offensive to the nameless new religion, and for a very simple reason. They encourage virtues the new faith explicitly rejects, such as chastity (no I won't move in unless you marry me), self-sacrifice (we'll stay together for the sake of the kids), obedience (I think dad's wrong, but I'll do what he says) and loyalty (it may be old-fashioned but I'm still going to church). These the new religion finds not just foolish but threatening. For virtues, if left unchecked, inevitably create over time all those in-dependent authorities the new faith has spent several centuries subverting and subduing: churches, private charities and hospi-tals, parent-run schools and little family businesses (L. Byfield 1999, 21).

But secular humanism is wrong. God (that is, the God of the Bible) exists, and this has social and political implications.

> The universe is not governed by hostile, impersonal forces, as the new religion says, but by an omnipotent Person who is, in a terrifyingly inscrutable and intolerant way, perfectly loving and infinitely giving. Not only did He give us life, He also gave us free-dom. That freedom brings with it awesome possibilities for both good and evil affecting everyone and everything around us. And the freedom amounts to this: to do as He wants, or to do as we want—and with all respect to the new faith, the two are not the same. Evil comes easily, goodness does not. It needs help, espe-

cially from free institutions such as the family. For the family, like creation itself, is founded ultimately upon self-sacrifice, not self-interest (L. Byfield 1999, 22).

Clearly, Link Byfield was a staunch conservative who believed strongly in individual freedom as well as traditional Western morality. This perspective was deeply rooted in Christianity. In fact, one cannot properly understand Link's conservative philosophy without appreciating its Christian basis. The same, of course, is true of his father, Ted.

CHAPTER 16

WESTERN REGIONALISM IN THE THOUGHT OF TED BYFIELD

Ted Byfield is deeply patriotic, particularly towards the Canada he knew as a child and young man. Unfortunately, the country has become severely deformed since that time. This helps to explain why sometimes he expresses a stirring national patriotism, but more often evidences a form of regional patriotism rooted in the West. In reality, the two are interrelated. Canada's original cultural identity seems to have lingered longer in the West, and that accounts for some of his deep-seated love for this region.

Another source of his commitment to the West is best expressed by his pithy statement, "Where your address is, there will your heart be also" (Byfield 1981c, 60). Bible readers will immediately recognize this as a variation on Jesus' words in Matthew 6:21 where He said, "For where your treasure is, there will your heart be also." Byfield's version is a common sense observation that people normally identify with the place where they live. People tend to cheer for the home team.

Defending western political rights is one of the three major features of Byfield conservatism. It is the purpose of this chapter to examine the western regionalist aspect of Byfield conservatism.

What is Canada's National Heritage?

First, however, it's worth looking at Ted Byfield's perception of Canada at its best. The liberal attack on what's best about Canada and Canadian identity has contributed to a weakening of the psychological ties that formerly bound westerners to the country at large. As the country has moved away from its historically based identity, it becomes harder for some westerners to recognize it.

Ted Byfield wrote the best description of Canada's national heritage ever. What does it mean to be a Canadian? For the Toronto arts and media community it means being ashamed of our history, opposing traditional morality and supporting an ever larger and more powerful government. But that view is rooted in modern ideology, not in the reality of Canada's past.

To provide a corrective, Ted Byfield wrote the following passage that really fills a void in providing an accurate brief description of genuine Canadian identity, at least for those who live in western Canada:

> *For what, when you get right down to it, is the national heritage? How did we get here? Are we not a people who crossed the seas, pushed back the forests, charted the rivers and lakes, rammed the railways through the mountains, broke the prairies, and tamed the barrens of the Arctic? Are we not a people who found gold in the Pre-Cambrian, oil in the Beaufort, and grew food for the world where men could hitherto scarcely find food enough for themselves?*
>
> *Are we French? Are we English? We are both, and German, Polish, Ukrainian, Dutch, Chinese and who knows what else. Why did we come here? For most, there was a single answer: land. For land, the Carignan-Solieres Regiment established the first substantial settlement in Quebec. For land, the Loyalists came. For land, the eastern Europeans peopled the western prairie. For land, the Chinese built with their blood the railways, the Japanese opened the fishery, and the Jews of Russia created Winnipeg's north end and the thousand cultural endeavours that have flowed from it. What all these people wanted, in other words, was private property, safe from expropriation, safe from tax collectors, safe from thief and marauder. Property, that is, meant freedom, and freedom was worth life itself.*
>
> *What did we believe? We believed in God. Religion was either*

the chief motive for, or indispensable companion of, almost every settlement. It was both puritanical and authoritarian, be it the authority of the Bible or the authority of the church. It was narrow, intolerant of non-conformity, and quick to condemn what it viewed as corruptive. But it was not anti-intellectual. Religion, in fact, established our school system. And a tough system it was, sparing neither rod nor child. It knew its goals, and against them it examined pupil and teacher remorselessly, overworking both. Indeed, work was a thing it revelled in, lots of it, with back and brain, dawn till long past darkness, men, women and children included. If a man would work, he should live. If he would not work, he should starve. If he could not work, it was up to the community to care for him, generously and positively with the hope that he would one day care for himself.

With the faith came the family. In families we arrived. In families we divided the land. In families we saw our children grow and prosper. In families we found companionship, purpose, comfort, warmth, guidance and an occasional clout on the ear. Was the mother of this family exploited and oppressed? She certainly was. Being exploited and oppressed was at once her burden, her privilege and her delight. That's what motherhood was about. In fact, in a sense, that's what the whole family was about. Either you believed in it, or you didn't.

We believed in it so much we quite readily fought for it, whether in the schoolyard or in the trenches. For we are indeed a fighting nation. Scarcely had the first shots been fired when we plunged into two world wars, years before the Americans, and those years we spent berating them for their backsliding cowardice. We left our blood and bones on the slopes of Vimy Ridge until we had hacked our way to the top of it, something the army of no other nation had been able to do. We were tied to posts and bayoneted at Hong Kong. We tore through the skies in the Battle of Britain, and we littered Germany with the corpses of our bomber crews. But these were wars of justice and we won them. We do not apologize for this (Byfield 1986a, 60).

This inspiring passage provides a powerful summary of the motivations that propelled Canada's history and the national character it developed. It is based on pride in our country's past and does not even attempt to cater to modern sensibilities. But this concept of Canada is out of fashion and certainly out of favour with the national political elites. Pierre Trudeau had much to do with undermining this historical view of Canada.

Why Alberta Became Angry in the 1970s and 1980s

Under Prime Minister Pierre Trudeau, Canada went through significant cultural and economic changes. Trudeau did not like the kind of Canada described by Ted Byfield. And it was largely due to Trudeau that many westerners developed a dislike for the central Canada that Trudeau represented.

Although there has probably been some sense of Western alienation since the earliest days of settlement, it boiled over from the 1970s through to the early 1990s. As mentioned, the policies and attitude of Prime Minister Trudeau had much to do with this. His successor, Brian Mulroney, simply added fuel to the fire.

Many people in the West, and especially in Alberta, came to believe that Confederation was rigged in favour of Ontario and Quebec. No one could explain this feeling better than Ted Byfield.

When the country was created, the provinces were given control over natural resources. Revenues from the development and sale of those resources belonged to the province. That was the accepted situation.

However, right from the beginning, federal economic policy encouraged industrial and commercial development primarily in southern Ontario and Quebec. Those areas also held the bulk of the country's population, which meant that they elected most members of parliament and thus controlled the government. Large-scale industrial development and most financial resources were concentrated in central Canada, but at least the hinterland provinces controlled their own natural resources.

However, largely due to events in the Middle East, the price of oil increased dramatically during the 1970s. The system was now poised to make Alberta very rich. However, Prime Minister Pierre Trudeau's government decided to change the rules. Byfield succinctly describes the situation this way:

> First it applied an export tax on oil—Canada had never before charged an export tax on anything—neatly siphoning off the added revenue to the federal treasury, and using the revenues to reduce the price of oil in Toronto and Montreal.

Then in 1980 the Trudeau government won election, with the full support of the Conservative government of Ontario, by promising to impose federal taxes directly on Alberta resources. This, of course, was against the law. But how do you "arrest" the federal government? The tax men entered the oil company offices and applied the taxes. Were these companies supposed to bar the doors? They had no option but to pay.

So the rules of the Canada game were now to be changed. They were sacrosanct only so long as Ontario and Quebec won by them. If the game started to go badly, you changed the rules. Alberta must learn to "share" with the rest of Canada, said Trudeau's energy minister, Marc Lalonde. Well, therefore, would a federal tax be levied on Quebec Hydro exports? Would Quebec be required to "share" its electric power with Nova Scotia, which depended on oil-fuelled thermal generators? Well no, that was a very different matter.

More and more it began to look as though Canada was a mere con game, being played out by Ontario and Quebec at the expense of the West. And the numbers proved it. Between 1969 and 1984, Alberta transferred more than $95 billion to the rest of Canada, most of it to Quebec, which gained $80 billion out of tax transfers and energy benefits during the same period. This money, had it remained in Alberta, would have financed industrial diversification in the bust that followed. But by then the money was gone (Byfield 1991, 3).

It was during this period that a separatist MLA was elected in a by-election in Alberta. Premier Peter Lougheed won tremendous support across the province by standing up for Alberta and threatening to cut off oil supplies to central Canada. "The Canadian flag was hauled down from hundreds of homes and some buildings and the Alberta flag raised instead" (Byfield 1991, 4).

All of Alberta's seats returned Progressive Conservative MPs in the federal election of 1984 which led to the government of Prime Minister Brian Mulroney. But Mulroney's government dragged its feet in repealing Trudeau's National Energy Program (NEP), and by then the oil industry was in dire straits. Mulroney's government subsequently awarded an aircraft maintenance contract that had been won by a Winnipeg company to a Montreal firm. Byfield writes: "Albertans recognized the symptoms. It didn't matter which party was in power at Ottawa. Unless the rules were changed, the West would be exploited permanently" (Byfield 1991, 4).

Byfield believed that the rule change needed was a reform of Canada's Senate so that it would represent provincial interests. In particular, he advocated the creation of a "Triple-E" Senate:

> By instituting a Senate in which all provinces were Equally repre-
> sented, which was Elected, and which was Effective in that it could
> veto the Commons. With such a Triple-E Senate in place, the NEP
> would never have been proposed, let alone passed. This was the
> protection which the Canadian constitution denied. This must be
> the West's objective (Byfield 1991, 4).

Two developments made the idea of promoting Senate reform realistic in the early 1990s. For one, Quebec wanted changes in the constitution, since it had not signed on in 1982. And secondly, the Reform Party of Canada was formed under the leadership of Preston Manning. Manning wanted the new party to be a positive force. As Byfield relates it,

> No longer would the West talk about "getting out of Canada." In-
> stead the slogan became, "The West Wants In," a phrase coined by
> Alberta Report columnist Ralph Hedlin. It means that the West
> wants constitutional changes that will enable it to play a more
> equal role in Canadian affairs, notably a Triple-E Senate (Byfield
> 1991, 5).

Thus the original anger developed in Alberta as a result of the oil crisis eventually played an important role in the emergence of the Reform Party of Canada. Unfortunately, the Reform Party was later dissolved into the Canadian Alliance which subsequently merged with the Progressive Conservative Party of Canada in 2003 to form the Conservative Party of Canada. As a result, the West lost a powerful tool for influence at the federal level.

Western Report magazine

Besides needing a political vehicle, the West needed a media voice. Developing such a distinctively western voice in the media to express the interests of the West was a goal of the Byfields' publishing enterprise.

Alberta Report magazine had originated as the St. John's Edmonton Report in 1973. A few years later the St. John's Calgary Report was added. In 1979 the two city magazines combined to form Alberta Report. Then at the beginning of 1986, the Western Report magazine was added as a companion to *Alberta Report* for the three other western provinces.

There were good business reasons to create *Western Report*. Because much of the content would be the same as the Alberta edition, only a few additional editors and writers were needed. The same production crew and facilities could produce the new magazine. Thus with only a small increase in costs, there was a potentially large increase in the market for the magazine with a corresponding increase in advertising revenues.

However, Ted Byfield also expressed non-monetary reasons for the new magazine. For one, he argued that the West needed to develop a regional perspective and viewpoint to encompass the common cause of western political interests. It must also embrace that cause to advance its economic interests.

On top of that, however, was a conservative ideological purpose. The West, more than other regions of Canada, still held to the foundational beliefs of the country's founders, and it needed a magazine to represent these beliefs. As Byfield put it:

> [W]e stand closer than any of the other regions to our pioneer roots. For most of us the farm is but one generation behind. We are therefore closer than they to the beliefs and traditions of the past, and we have the advantage of seeing what happens when those values are too hurriedly cast aside in favour of a state-centred secularism of glittering promise and baleful result. It is a view not well represented in the contemporary media of the West, an omission we propose to correct (Byfield 1985b, 52).

Thus one significant purpose of *Western Report* was to uphold and maintain the conservative perspectives and traditions still held in western Canada.

Alberta history series

Alberta Report and its sister magazines frequently faced financial difficulties. Without financial infusions from sympathetic donors, it likely would have folded. There was one particular financial success, however. Beginning in the early 1990s, the magazine also began producing a 12-volume history set called "Alberta in the 20th Century." This project was surprisingly profitable and produced much needed revenue to keep the magazines afloat.

The success of this popular history series was counterintuitive. Byfield attributed this success, in part, to the emergence of an Alberta identity. He wrote,

> There is gradually developing in Alberta a very powerful provincial identity. Perhaps it's because we have so often been called "redneck" by the rest of Canada, perhaps because we have so often resisted trends in the rest of Canada, perhaps because we live closer to our frontier origins, perhaps because from our very beginning almost everything we produce must be sold on a world market, not a protected local one. And, finally, perhaps because our national identity has become so confused of late that it's hard to define what being a Canadian is supposed to mean. There's little doubt what being an Albertan means, and this has a deepening significance. That, we believe, is one of the chief reasons for the success of the history series (Byfield 1999, 2).

The meaning of Canadian identity that Byfield expressed so clearly in 1986 was continuing to fade. Thus the Alberta identity was emerging more strongly than ever. His Alberta history series likely contributed to the increasing strength of that identity as well.

Finding the West's place in Canada

Ted Byfield's Alberta patriotism has been on display since the late 1970s. Indeed, during Alberta's showdown With Prime Minister Pierre Trudeau over oil pricing and the National Energy Program, he was front and centre fighting for Alberta (Wagner, 2009). He would later play a key role in the formation of the Reform Party of Canada, as has been mentioned.

After the Reform Party had folded into the Canadian Alliance, Byfield continued to press for western interests to be asserted in Canada. The 2000 federal election left many westerners frustrated that the East had once again voted overwhelmingly for the Liberal Party. Separatist sentiment began to emerge in Alberta anew.

Byfield wrote some columns on different options the West could follow under those circumstances. The West could just accept the status quo, or it could follow the route proposed by Stephen Harper's "Alberta Agenda," or it could attempt real reform. Byfield favoured the third option, which he attributed to Gordon Gibson, the former leader of the BC Liberal Party. The third option involved threatening to separate from Canada as a way to get concessions from the rest of the country.

This is how he argued the point:

> Unless we make credible threats to set up on our own we will get absolutely nothing by way of constitutional change, or any other kind of change. We will be bashed down every time. If we threatened to leave and meant it, we would have enormous clout in Canada, more even than Quebec. By refusing to entertain such an idea, we have no clout whatever. That is the message of history—and of the last three federal elections.
>
> So am I advocating separatism? No (Byfield 2001, 60).

He goes on to explain that separatism is just a threat that would make the rest of Canada take the West's demands seriously and thus lead to beneficial reforms.

> We should go back to the negotiating table, just as Quebec is proposing to do, and we should go back as Quebec goes back—with other options clearly in view—such as an independent state, or joining the American union. If we go to the table with these alternatives thoroughly explored, tenable and widely understood, we will come away with quite a bit, and a very new Canada will emerge. If we go to the table without those options, we will come away with nothing whatever. All central Canada need do is stymie the negotiational process and we will have to slump back into the status quo as we always have.
>
> In other words, we are presented with a paradox. The only way we can change Canada is to develop ways of getting out of Canada. We must possess other options (Byfield 2001, 2).

Clearly, Byfield did not really want the West to pull out of Canada to form its own country. But he saw the threat to do so as the only viable option to make central Canada sit up and take the West's demands seriously. Threatening to pull out was largely a negotiating strategy. But it was supported by a firm commitment to the West's best interests and a recognition that the West could do better on its own.

Advocating for the interests of the West is clearly a central tenet of the Byfield conservative perspective.

CHAPTER 17

PARENTAL RIGHTS IN THE THOUGHT OF TED BYFIELD

In the modern culture war between social conservatives and social left-ists, one of the most intensely fought battles is over parental rights. Who should exercise control over the upbringing of children, parents or the state? This issue brings the culture war directly into the home and is of overwhelming significance to many parents. Parents who uphold traditional morality are especially involved in this issue. Byfield conservatism is unabashedly and fully committed to parental rights.

Ted Byfield was deeply involved in the St. John's private Christian schools in Manitoba and Alberta, so it is not surprising that he valued parental rights in education as well as educational freedom. In fact, as editor of *Alberta Report* and its sister magazines, parental rights were a consistent and persistent theme of his columns. No other writer in western Canada, and perhaps the entire country, provided constant support for parental rights and constant criticism of the left-wing activists, politicians, and government bureaucrats who wanted to extend the power of the state over the family. The family is a pillar of society, in the Christian view, and it was always upheld by the materials Ted Byfield published.

From the late 1970s through the 1980s, Alberta experienced considerable controversy over private education (Wagner 1995). Thankfully, Ted Byfield was on the scene to articulate and explain the concerns and perspectives of parents.

In 1980 the *Edmonton Journal* published a front page story that supposedly "exposed" the shortcomings of Centennial Montessori, a private school in Edmonton. Some of the staff had different qualifications than would normally be held by public school staff. As well, the classroom hours and facilities were quite different from that of the public schools. Available test results indicated that the students were doing well but that was beside the point. The *Journal* claimed that the education of children in all schools was a government responsibility.

Ted Byfield argued strongly against that view and in favor of educational freedom. In defending the Montessori school he took on both the *Journal* and the Alberta Teachers' Association (ATA). He wrote:

> *Is your child primarily your responsibility or is your child primarily a "public" responsibility, which is to say a responsibility of the state? There is a strong tradition in our society, going back to the roots of antiquity, that the parent—not the state—is primarily responsible for the education of a child. Obviously the parents who send their children to the Montessori school do so because they prefer that kind of education for their children. If they are dissatisfied, they can take their children out and send them somewhere else.*
>
> *But the teachers' union has apparently decided that parents are too stupid to make such a decision. It wants to "protect" children from the irresponsibilities of their own parents. It joins with the jackals at the* Journal *to demand that independent education be subject to "controls." It knows, of course, that the whole point of independent education is that it is independent: the state does not control it. Making it subject to state control is therefore one way of getting rid of it, which the ATA would dearly like to do. The absurdity of the state controlling independent schools when its own are so obviously out of control apparently does not occur to it (Byfield 1980a, 52).*

Previously in his column, Byfield had referred to a series of articles in the *Edmonton Journal* that had described a thriving market for illegal drugs in Alberta's public schools. He also referenced a recent report received by the Calgary Board of Education on the high rate of sexual activity among its students. This was the background to his comment about the government's own schools being "out of control."

Religious motive for private schools

A year later Byfield wrote another column defending independent schools from the three entrenched establishments of the public education system: the bureaucrats at the provincial government and school board levels, the university faculties of education, and the teachers' unions. All three groups feel threatened by private schools.

The increasing demand for independent schools at that time in Alberta was driven by parents. Byfield wrote that the parents had three main complaints about the public education system. First, they think the public schools are failing academically. They were concerned that academic standards were falling. Secondly, they believed that discipline was no longer properly being enforced in the schools. Thirdly, public schools had been adopting an educational philosophy that was unacceptable to many parents.

Byfield described the philosophical differences this way:

> *Most parents were either specifically or at least vaguely Christian. They believed in a God who through a process of revelation had endowed human beings with a sense of right and wrong, generally formulated in ten commandments, enlarged upon by the Hebrew prophets, and exemplified in the life of Christ. The school system on the other hand preached a liberal humanism that rendered God largely irrelevant and made man himself the final object of all human endeavour (Byfield 1981a, 52).*

The entrenched establishments listed above had two main arguments against private schools. First, they believed a proliferation of such schools would lead to social division and conflict because the province's children would not be learning together in common schools. Secondly, they were concerned that wealthy parents would send their children to elite schools that could provide privileged children with a superior education. This would mean some children got a better start in life than the others. To them, that's not fair.

Byfield, however, suspected that another concern was driving the opposition to private schools:

> *The advance in independent education has been sponsored almost entirely from religious motive. What the independent schools therefore represent is a challenge, not only to public education but to the philosophy that underlies public education. Their wide-*

spread success would imply a great deal more than an educational accomplishment. It would expose the general impoverishment of liberal humanism itself, and constitute a vindication of the religious position. And that would be intolerable (Byfield 1981a, 52).

In this sense the opposition to the growth of private education was partly fuelled by antagonism to conservative Christianity. The culture war loomed large.

The Jones case

One of the most significant events in the debate over private education in Alberta during the 1980s was the "Jones case." Pastor Larry Jones of Western Baptist Church in Calgary opened a private school but refused to apply for a government license. In his view, God required him to educate his own children, and he didn't need to get the government's permission (i.e. a license) to do what God had commanded him to do. He refused the license as a matter of religious principle.

The government took Jones to court. At the initial court level Jones won, but the government appealed and scored a victory at the Alberta Court of Appeal. Jones then appealed to the Supreme Court of Canada, which ruled against him in October 1986. As Ted Byfield pointed out, Jones' loss was a loss for parental rights in general:

For what has been decided here, it becomes plain, is that the right of the state shall supersede the right of the parent in deciding what constitutes an adequate education. If a minority group of parents decides they do not agree with the way the state wants to educate their children, and that they will therefore do it themselves, then the state will have the right to move in, take their children away from them, and educate them to the state's liking (Byfield 1986b, 52).

The implications of this decision were very favourable to the desires of the teachers' unions. Byfield explained why:

If the state can decide who may run a school, then it falls implicit that the state can also decide who may teach—not just within its own school system, but in any school, of any type, anywhere. This has long been the aim of the teachers' unions. They want to be "professionals," like doctors, they say. "Would you let a non-professional take out a child's appendix? Why, therefore, would you let a non-professional teach a child to read?" Such is the argument (Byfield 1986b, 52).

Moving in the direction of recognizing teaching as a profession, then, would clearly limit the freedom of parents to make alternative educational choices for their children. Homeschooling would be especially threatened. But the success of "non-professionals," like mothers, teaching children how to read, clearly demonstrates that the teachers' unions should not be given the status of professionals.

Fundamental flaw of public education

A couple of years later an Alberta public school principal cancelled his subscription to *Alberta Report* and included a letter explaining his reason for the cancellation. He said the magazine was constantly carping about the deficiencies of the public school system without acknowledging that the difficulties were just a matter of a few problem schools and problem teachers here and there.

Byfield acknowledged that the magazine was regularly criticizing the public schools. But he said the problems were not just the result of schools and teachers here and there. The situation was much more serious than that. As he put it, "I think the system is fundamentally flawed, flawed in its philosophy, and flawed most of all in its view of human nature, and consequently of the children who come within its care. I think its problems are, therefore, not incidental but symptomatic" (Byfield 1988c, 48).

He went into detail about the basic flaw as follows:

More than any institution of government, the public schools in the 1950s and 1960s underwent a convulsive change. It was not mere renovation or rehabilitation. It was a total revolution, a change of goals, assumptions, methods and expectations. Above all it involved a changed view of humanity. No longer were we made in the image of God, creatures endowed with a free will, capable of good, but prone to ill, determining our destiny by the way we lived to be either an ultimate heaven and an ultimate hell. Instead we became mere biological throw-offs, the products of a mechanical process of unknowable purpose. No longer was it we ourselves who determined our behaviour: our psychology determined it for us. How could we, therefore, be held responsible for what we did? Personal gratification became the highest human goal, physical

> *survival the central social aspiration, and good and bad anything*
> *anybody wanted to make them. Obviously the change from the*
> *former view to the latter must result in a radically different meth-*
> *od of education, and that is the change we have seen occur (By-*
> *field 1988c, 48).*

In his view, it was this change in the underlying perspective of public education that provided the key impetus for the growth of private education.

Corporal punishment

Besides education, another major area of contention over parental rights is the corporal punishment of children. Parents have the legal right to spank children as a form of punishment. This is an outrage to many leftists who view all corporal punishment, no matter how mild or loving, to be child abuse.

In the late 1990s a "children's rights" organization called the Canadian Foundation for Children, Youth and the Law, launched a Charter challenge to section 43 of the Criminal Code which provides the legal basis for corporal punishment. That organization argued that section 43 violated the Charter of Rights and Freedoms by denying children equal protection of the law. Adults are protected from all forms of violence, so equal treatment would provide children with the same protection, thereby criminalizing spanking.

The case went all the way to the Supreme Court of Canada. Thankfully, on January 30, 2004, the court upheld section 43, so spanking remained legal within limits.

When the challenge was first launched, Ted Byfield wrote a column explaining the deficiency in the "children's rights" argument. He pointed out that it is completely reasonable to deny children certain rights and that this is widely recognized:

> *Of course, children are deprived of other rights not mentioned by*
> *the foundation. They may not vote. They are denied liquor and*
> *cigarettes. Sexual activity among them is discouraged, and sex*
> *with an adult prohibited by yet another Criminal Code section.*
> *They are forced to attend school. They are sadly restricted in the*
> *matter of credit cards, and ruthlessly prohibited from driving an*
> *automobile. The list of discriminatory curtailments on "the rights*
> *of the child" is practically limitless.*

Now the reason is simply this: The child is regarded, indeed is described in law, as "a dependent." Because children are deemed unable to realistically foresee the consequences of what they're doing (a disability many might attribute to the foundation as well) they are denied the rights to such things as tobacco, drugs, sex, credit cards, automobiles and freedom from education.

Therefore the child is seen to be "dependent" on its parents. Should the parents shirk this responsibility the law holds them culpable. But another ancient principle of justice applies here. Society must not confer a responsibility without conferring sufficient authority to carry it out. You cannot expect a man or woman to do something unless they have the power to do it. That's why the Criminal Code recognizes this right of parents, teachers and legal guardians to physically discipline children—and why the parliamentarians won't snatch it away.

So the foundation's case is not really about children being denied a right. Children are denied all kinds of rights. Neither is it fundamentally about law. It's about child-raising—the philosophy and practicality of parenting—and let's hope, however dim the prospect, the court sees it that way (Byfield 1998a, 44).

Thankfully, the court did see it that way. The good guys won for a change. And the case provided the opportunity for Ted Byfield to explain the case for corporal punishment in a way that even some leftists could understand.

CHAPTER 18

LEGISLATION AND MORALITY IN THE THOUGHT OF TED BYFIELD

In the early years of the culture war, social conservatives were frequently accused of wanting to "legislate morality." This was especially true regarding the issues of abortion and homosexual rights. There's a sense in which the charge is true because all legislation is the enforcement of some concept of morality. The leftists want to legislate their morality as well.

Traditional morality is at the center of conflicts in the culture war, and it is a key plank of Byfield conservatism.

Conflicting belief systems

In 1985 the Canadian Civil Liberties Association mailed out a letter designed to recruit more supporters to its cause. The letter was written by Dalton Camp (the back-stabber of John Diefenbaker), and it purported to warn Canadians about the dangerous political activities of evangelical Christians in Canada and the United States.

Ted Byfield used the controversy surrounding Camp's letter to explain an important point about conflicting belief systems. If someone accepts a particular belief system, the logical corollary is that other belief systems are false. If something is true, then opposing ideas are false. As Byfield put it:

> *The instant you accept any religious statement as true, you are compelled to reject anything incompatible with that statement as*

false. If I were to become a Muslim, for instance, I would have to believe that Jesus Christ was not crucified, since that is the assertion of the Holy Koran. I would therefore have to reject as false the Christian assertion that he was crucified. To believe Islam a true religion means believing Christianity, insofar as it disagrees with Islam, a false one. Similarly, to be a Roman Catholic means believing Protestantism in certain particulars to be a false religion, and believing in Judaism means believing both Islam and Christianity in certain aspects to be false religions (Byfield 1985a, 60).

This might sound obvious but it needs to be stated plainly. Many leftists claim it is "intolerant" to say that any particular religion is a false religion. And since Canada is a supposedly very "tolerant" society, saying such things is alarming and distasteful. Some would even like to criminalize such speech to allegedly stamp out "hate." But the implications of doing so are very serious. Byfield explains as follows:

To believe anything true is to believe that which is incompatible with it false. If it is "intolerant" to call another religion false, then of course it must be equally intolerant to call your own religion true. And if it were made illegal to call a religion false, this would surely imply it must be illegal to call a religion true. If A is true, then B must be false. If it is illegal to call B false, then it must also be illegal to call A true (Byfield 1985a, 60).

Many civil liberties supporters see religion as a "personal affair" that must be kept out of political matters. Religion must be private, not public.

And when religion is publicly advanced as some sort of universal truth, they say, the pages of man's history turn blood red with the wars and persecutions that result. And since evangelicals are the people most distinguished for publicly and loudly asserting it, the spectacle of an active evangelism, demanding a voice for Christian moral teaching in the legislative process, is exceedingly repugnant. As a scare image, it is therefore especially useful in recruiting new members to the civil liberties cause. And that is why the letter was written (Byfield 1985a, 60).

Byfield explains the problem with the objective of many of the leftists who hold this view:

The danger is that these rights and liberties people have a seemingly irresistible yen to legislate. Calling a thing bad isn't enough. There must always be a law against it. Now they are on to what

> is known as "hate literature." They want the laws against it "strengthened." Will someone please say no. For if the Muslims aren't allowed to call my religion false, and I theirs, then both of us will very soon find ourselves denied the right to call our own beliefs true, and we'll both be the losers. Let's leave the laws as they are, and stick to the devil we know (Byfield 1985a, 60).

The leftists who are supposedly against "intolerance" and "hate" are the ones who want to use the coercive power of the state to suppress opinions they don't like. This is a very clear example of where they would like to legislate their own morality at the cost of freedom and open discussion.

Legislating Morality

In 1981 the *Edmonton Journal* obtained a new editor-in-chief, Stephen Hume. Hume wrote an editorial condemning Christian involvement in political matters, specifically Rev. Jerry Falwell and his organization, the Moral Majority. At that time, both Falwell and the Moral Majority were powerful actors in American politics and considered to be the vanguard of the Christian Right. In Hume's view, they were "pushing people around on behalf of God" because they desired legislation in accordance with their beliefs.

It is true, of course, that Christian groups like Moral Majority do want legislation in accordance with their beliefs. This is condemned by liberals as the imposition of morality upon other people. In a sense that's true too. But it's also true that liberals want their morality imposed by law, so they are guilty of the very thing they accuse the conservative Christian groups of doing. This is a point that Ted Byfield explained at some length:

> [W]hen Christians say they believe that God wills something, they mean among other things that it is morally right. Not simply right for themselves, but right universally. Believing the family to be good, they believe also that those things which erode the institution of the family are wrong. Believing the body to be the tabernacle of the spirit, they believe also that its exploitation whether by prostitution, pornography or over-indulgence is wrong, not just for themselves but universally. That is why for nearly two thousand years they have helped to shape the law, and they will no doubt continue to do so, however distasteful to liberal newspaper editors.

> But the liberals, of course, have their morality too, which they

> *advance with all the certitude of a Jerry Falwell or a St. Augustine. Notice that when a moral principle is asserted by a Christian—touching, for instance, on abortion or on the sanctity of the family—the* Journal *inevitably sees this as an expression of mere personal "taste," being "imposed" by Christians on those who do not accept Christianity. But when the principle asserted touches on such things as the responsibility of the state to care for the unfortunate, or on racial tolerance, or on the "rights" of women, or on a hundred other liberal causes, suddenly morality has acquired much stronger credentials. No longer is it mere taste or opinion. It has now become right, and right for everybody. But how does the* Journal *know it is right? They never do say (Byfield 1981b, 52).*

In short, the liberals want legislation to reflect their morality. What they criticize in others is the very thing they engage in themselves.

> *Hence the same newspaper whose editor deplores those who invoke a higher principle as an authority for their views itself invokes such principles day by day. It does not tell us that in the* Journal's *"taste and opinion" this or that policy would be right. It asserts its views with the full force of universal moral rightness as well it should. For why else should we pay the least head to what the Journal says? But the difference between, say, Mr. Falwell and the* Journal *is that Mr. Falwell has figured this out and the* Journal *hasn't (Byfield 1981b, 52).*

A few years later Byfield took up this same basic issue with the *Globe and Mail*. Jeffrey Simpson's coverage of the 1996 Republican convention was full of language condemning the Religious Right and the Christian Coalition, the leading organization of the Christian Right at that time. The Coalition was allegedly violating the separation of church and state by advocating that people should have their theology inform their political views.

Byfield clearly laid out the hypocritical implication of the stance taken by the *Globe*:

> *All law, whether criminal or civil, is the enactment of some moral principle. The citizen therefore takes his stand on any proposed law on the basis of whatever moral code he accepts. If he derives his morality from liberal professors, the movies, the newspapers, or last week's episode of Law and Order, that's fine. But if he derives it from the Bible or the Koran or the teachings of the Church,*

that's wrong. He's violating the separation of church and state. Only possible conclusion: All Christians, Muslims and religious Jews should not vote and should stay out of politics (Byfield 1996c, 44).

It seems that that, indeed, may be the preferred outcome of many leftists. They could impose their own morality on the country without any opposition. But for all people, political opinions are informed by their morality, so keeping morality out of politics would mean that there would be no politics at all, an obvious impossibility.

Homosexuality

In recent decades the clash between Christian and secular conceptions of morality has been especially sharp over the issues of abortion and homosexual rights. These were matters that Ted Byfield did not avoid. In fact, he tackled them head-on numerous times in his columns.

In 1996 the Canadian Human Rights Act was amended to add sexual orientation as a protected category. This was a significant victory for homosexual rights activists and something that Byfield (and many others) strongly opposed. He reminded readers of the reason for traditional morality and the reason it was being discarded:

Morality serves always as a restraint on human desire, which usually means on human aggression. When you remove the morality, therefore, you remove the restraint. And it is this, not any new scientific or moral enlightenment, that accounts for our revision of attitude. The rules inhibited us, so we got rid of the rules. No longer must women bear the children conceived within them. No longer need men or women heed vows of sexual exclusivity. No longer need these ancient curbs against sodomy, bestiality, pederasty and other assorted sexual delights confine and restrict us. So we steadily rid ourselves of the laws, and then make it illegal for anyone to oppose or criticize what we have done (Byfield 1996a, 44).

Criticism of homosexuality is certainly considered to be in bad taste by the political and media establishment today. And in some contexts it can trigger government action against the critic through a so-called "human rights" commission.

Byfield went on to correctly identify some of the results of extending homosexual rights through legislation:

> *It will mean that parents will find their school children being
> lectured on the beauties of sodomy and other proclivities by
> representatives of the "gay community," and if they try to stop
> it, they will be branded as "bigots" and "hate-mongers" and
> threatened with prosecution (Byfield 1996a, 44).*

Anyone currently speaking out against the advance of the homosexual
rights crusade in public schools would likely be able to attest to the truth
of that statement.

Byfield also correctly predicted that homosexual couples would be able
to adopt children (they can't produce children together through normal,
biological methods) and opponents would, of course, be accused of "hatred." And he was concerned that it would become "against the law to
read out loud in any public place those passages in the Bible that condemn" sodomy, since that, too, would be declared to be "hatred."

Abortion

From early on Ted Byfield was a spokesman for the pro-life cause. He
has been an outspoken defender of unborn children. In one instance he
was asked by the CBC to be on a television program with the infamous
abortionist Dr. Henry Morgentaler. In the course of this program Byfield presented Morgentaler with a particular hypothetical situation of
the kind social studies teachers were being encouraged to present to their
students:

> *Several men are out in the woods hunting. Suddenly one of them
> sees something move in the bush. At last, he rejoices, a deer. Then
> a warning flashes through his mind. That might not be a deer.
> That might be one of the other hunters. Question for the class:
> Should the hunter fire at the thing if there's a chance it's another
> human being? The approved answer is no (Byfield 1980b, 44).*

After posing his question the television program was never run and he
was never invited back. Morgentaler was a CBC hero and Byfield's question exposed the wicked cause that he was promoting. The question may
have been considered unfair.

> *The question may be hypothetical but it is certainly not unfair.
> The doctor, along with other liberals who defend this hideous
> practice, in effect argues as follows: We do not know at what point
> during pregnancy a fetus or an embryo becomes, in fact, a human
> being—whether at the instant of conception, or at the instant of*

birth, or at some intervening stage. Because of this uncertainty, abortion may be permitted at some elementary phase of growth. In other words, since we do not know whether the thing is human or it isn't, then it is all right to kill it, the very reverse of the conclusion that sane people would reach in the case of the hunter. The moral principle must surely be: If you don't know, you don't kill it. The abortionist argues: If you don't know, you may (Byfield 1980b, 44).

At the time Byfield wrote that column, the town of Ponoka was known as the "Abortion Capital of Alberta" due to a hospital there that was congenial to the "procedure." Abortion had become widely accepted in Canadian society, but Byfield was convinced that in the future abortion would be recognized for its true nature:

We do not suspect that another age may recoil in horror at the whole spectacle of what we are doing, and condemn it as we condemn the grand scale slaughters worked by other establishments in other days who were equally confident of what they were doing. That would be a time when the mere mention of a grandfather who worked in such-and-such a hospital would occasion an awkward silence in the conversation, and when the name of a town called Ponoka would carry with it the same connotation as that of another town called Auschwitz (Byfield 1980b, 44).

Clearly, Byfield has long recognized that the mass killing of unborn children in Canada through abortion can rightfully be compared to other holocausts of the past.

Perhaps his clearest expression of the case against abortion was in the column he wrote in the immediate aftermath of the *Morgentaler* Supreme Court decision that was handed down at the end of January 1988. This decision struck down the provision of the Criminal Code that required abortions to be performed exclusively in hospitals that had Therapeutic Abortion Committees. Each committee was composed of three medical doctors who had to approve any request for an abortion.

Dr. Henry Morgentaler wanted to perform abortions in his own clinic in Toronto. When he did so, he was charged with violating the law. However, he won his case by arguing that the Criminal Code restrictions on abortion violated the Charter of Right's guarantee of "security of the person."

In condemning this decision, and arguing that Canada's Supreme Court had opened the door to "barbarism," Byfield clearly laid out the case against abortion in the form of three questions and answers:

Ought one human being have, as a matter of unchallengeable right, the exclusive "choice" of killing or not killing another human being?

The answer of all civilized societies: No.

What is the starting point of a human being?

The only possible answer: The point at which it acquires individuality, becomes either male or female, has hair, eyes and skin of a given colour, an endowed intelligence, a particular physical strength and form, an appetite, a way in which he or she will walk and talk, a certain way of smiling and a certain way of weeping, an age at which it will most likely turn into an adult, and a time at which it will most likely die.

When is that decided?

The answer of all genetic science is now unchallenged and unequivocal: It is decided at the instant of conception. The fertilized egg is like a computer chip. The genetic "program" to produce the person is already there.

Killing a fetus is therefore not merely dispensing with human waste. It is destroying a particular boy or girl, of particular characteristics, of particular potential for good or ill. What gets dumped into the garbage of abortion mills day in and day out is not a load of protoplasm. It is the remains of thousands of people. That is what science is saying, and it is saying it with clinical and unemotional accuracy (Byfield 1988a, 48).

With the *Morgentaler* decision, the barbarian was now within the gates of Canadian society. Byfield called on his readers to resist the barbarian at every point. Significantly, he added: "But we need remember we beat him the last time, not by force of arms but by force of words" (Byfield 1988a, 48).

From Christianity to secular humanism

In 1996 Trinity Western University (TWU), a Christian institution in BC, applied to the British Columbia College of Teachers (BCCT) to have its teacher training program certified. The BCCT rejected TWU's request because the university had a Community Standards document that obligates all students, staff and faculty to live according to Christian ethical standards. The BCCT deemed the document to be discriminatory against homosexuals because Christianity condemns homosexual behaviour.

To make a long story short, this case went all the way to the Supreme Court of Canada. In 2001 the Supreme Court decided in TWU's favour, although it was a qualified victory.

In the early stages of this conflict, Ted Byfield used it as an example of how Canada was changing. Originally Canada was a generally Christian country. Then it became a "pluralistic" country where all kinds of different religions and perspectives were allowed. But the TWU case showed that we actually weren't pluralistic after all. If Canada was truly pluralistic, then when TWU was refused accreditation because of its Christian beliefs the mainstream media would come out in its defence. But the media did not do so.

Pluralism, at best, is the transition stage as a society moves from one dominant worldview (or ideology) to another. As mentioned, Christianity was originally the dominant worldview in Canada. Then the country entered a pluralistic stage. Now the phase of pluralism is transitioning to a period of secular humanist dominance. Byfield explains the process as follows:

> In truth, we are not changing from an ideologically based society into a neutral one. We are adopting a new and very different ideology. Where certain forms of conduct consistent with Christianity were previously backed by the force of law, now other forms of conduct, very alien to Christianity, will be backed with equal (or greater) force. Where social stigma once attached to certain lifestyles—e.g., living common law, having an abortion, selling goods on Sunday—in the new society social stigma will attach to other sorts of things—e.g., making jokes about national or racial groups, denying access to abortion, hiring people on the basis of competence alone, suggesting that some forms of sexual behaviour are morally good and others bad (Byfield 1996b, 44).

Byfield used the TWU situation to illustrate that pluralism was not being practiced.

> In a pluralistic society, a Christian institution would maintain a Christian moral code, a Muslim institution a Muslim moral code, a secular institution a secular moral code, and so on. But in a society whose official ideology was secular humanism the secu-

lar code would be enforced on all institutions—which is precisely what is happening here. Unless TWU agrees to advance the secular code, it will not be allowed to qualify teachers. Thus we have the teachers' college, armed with power conferred upon it by the state, imposing secular views on a Christian institution. Pluralism has vanished (Byfield 1996b, 44).

As mentioned, TWU actually won the case at the Supreme Court level. However, the same university is now embroiled in a similar conflict over its proposed law school. A number of provincial law societies have refused to accept TWU graduates as lawyers due to the university's Christian code of conduct. Christian sexual morality is anathema to the law societies whose power has been conferred upon them by the state. The success of TWU's endeavours in accrediting its law school is very much in doubt. This would not be the case in a genuinely pluralistic society.

But it does illustrate, once again, that the Left is very comfortable legislating its morality and imposing its views on the rest of us. In a sense this is what the culture war is all about. Which morality will be legislated? Christian morality or secular humanist morality?

CHAPTER 19

THE IMPORTANCE OF RELIGION AND HISTORY IN THE THOUGHT OF TED BYFIELD

There can be no doubt that Christianity is the foundation of the whole Byfield perspective. Indeed, the *St. John's Edmonton Report* was founded as a newsmagazine with a Christian viewpoint, and that viewpoint continued to play a significant role throughout its life and its successor publications.

Most of the time the Christian perspective was implicit. Occasionally, however, Ted would write explicitly Christian columns. Indeed, together with Virginia, a column entitled "Orthodoxy" was introduced into the magazine in the early 1990s. The Byfields were not in the habit of hiding their Christian beliefs.

In 1980 American evangelist Billy Graham held a gospel crusade in Edmonton. *Alberta Report* gave the crusade good coverage. As well, Ted Byfield wrote a column endorsing the crusade. He wrote, "For Albertans this is an unparalleled opportunity to hear the foremost preacher in the English language of the late 20th century" (Byfield 1980c, 44).

Much of the column explains the liberal drift of Alberta society and the negative consequences that have resulted from that drift. He then described how Billy Graham's Christian outlook rejected such liberal ideas:

> *He has made it fairly clear in the past, for instance, that a good society depends chiefly upon there being good people, and that good people depend chiefly upon something he calls the grace of*

> God. A society that has rejected the grace of God in favor of various psychological, physiological and sociological substitutes can expect the kind of calamity that appears to be befalling this one. The solution does not lie in that case in various sociological formulae, nor in new drugs, nor in new legislative reforms, nor in firing [Minister of Social Services] Bob Bogle. The only remedy that will work is one that cures not the symptoms of our malaise, but its cause. The cause is spiritual. Dr. Graham has come here to deal with the cause (Byfield 1980c, 44).

And, of course, this was precisely Byfield's view as well, namely, that the fundamental problem of Alberta society was a spiritual problem. He thus concludes the column this way: "We welcome Billy Graham to Alberta. He is sorely needed" (Byfield 1980c, 44).

Defending evangelism

A few years later Byfield wrote a column defending the evangelization of Africa. An American televangelist had conducted crusades in West Africa and this had drawn the ire of the *Globe and Mail* newspaper. According to that newspaper, the West Africans were being "exploited" by the evangelistic crusades.

According to Byfield, the question was, what do the West Africans need most: food, agricultural technology and democracy? Or the Word of God? The Word of God is more important than the others because it leads to the others. That is, Christianization leads to economic and political development. This was how things played out in the West, at least. Byfield explains:

> What was it, after all, that brought about our educational establishment? What gave rise to our democratic institutions? Fourteen centuries ago, the western world was itself tribal. London was the desolate wreck of a one-time Roman provincial city, Paris a squalid accretion of mud-floored hovels, Germany the barren battlefield of a dozen or more barbarian hordes. We were the Third World of that day. And what did the First World send us that would really matter? Was it food, an end to our tribal warfare, agricultural technology, education, civilized institutions? Very conclusively not. What they sent was the "Word of God."

> The evangelists of those days had different names, of course. There were no Swaggerts [sic], no Billy Grahams. But there was a Boni-

face, a Patrick, an Alban, a Columba, a Methodius, and a thou-
sand others. Moreover, the Message was exactly the same; in a
millennium and a half it has not changed by one iota (Byfield
1987, 52).

With this in mind it is not surprising that West Africans would be flock-
ing to hear an American evangelist preach the gospel.

Perhaps they know, as we once did, that a man on his knees,
whether in a grass skirt or a business suit, who raises his hands
and says "praise God," or signs himself with the cross, or both, is
no longer just a man. In him flows the grace through which in
countless ages vast civilizations have come to be, and dazzling
scientific advance has been achieved. And perhaps they see, too,
that all these things are yet but shadows of greater glories that lie
beyond that which we can now touch and see (Byfield 1987, 52).

Clearly, the gospel constituted a greater priority to Ted Byfield than the
worldly benefits that flow from a society that embraces it.

The trial and execution of Jesus Christ

In 1965 Pierre Berton wrote a book called *The Comfortable Pew: A Crit-*
ical Look at Christianity and the Religious Establishment in the New Age.
Berton had been officially commissioned by the Anglican Church of
Canada to write this report, analyzing the current state of that church.
Berton did not attend church regularly and he held fashionably liberal
views about the issues of the day, and this was all reflected in the book. It
was a run-away best seller when it came out early in 1965 and it received
international attention.

Ted Byfield wrote a response to Berton called *Just Think, Mr. Berton (A*
Little Harder). Not only that, but he was invited to confront Berton on a
TV program. Byfield relates the occasion as follows:

Years ago I appeared on national television to defend Christian-
ity against Pierre Berton whose assault on it, The Comfortable
Pew, *had just been published. Mr. Berton made mincemeat of*
me, I have to admit, but in the course of our 10-minute encoun-
ter, I managed to point out that his book contains an appalling
misstatement of fact. It contends that Jesus was put to death on
charges of sedition. The sedition charge, in fact, was dropped be-
cause the witnesses disagreed. He was then placed under oath and
ordered to identify himself. He did so with the name of God, and

was thereupon sentenced to death for blasphemy. In talking with Mr. Berton after the program I found him plainly irritated, but not with me. "I showed that manuscript," he said, "to something like four clergymen at Church House in Toronto, and not one of them noticed that mistake. Why is this?" (Byfield 1988b, 56).

Byfield didn't know the answer to that question at the time, but he later came up with a theory. He doesn't think those clergymen had carefully read the account of Christ's trial and crucifixion. They didn't really know the details of the story.

In the same column relating his encounter with Pierre Berton on TV, Byfield recounts another interesting experience someone had when considering Christ and His life:

Some time in the 1920s a young Englishman named Frank Morison sat down to write a book on what actually happened in the two days before Jesus Christ was executed. He wanted to call it "Jesus: the Last Phase," and in it he planned to explain what likely took place in Christ's trial and execution, and how the "myth" of his resurrection had subsequently developed. Morison did not write this book, and for a compelling reason. The more closely he examined the accounts, along with what is known of contemporary Jewish history and practice, the more he became convinced that only one thesis would fit all the facts, notably the one the accounts themselves advanced. The man must have risen bodily from the dead. This conclusion he published in 1930 under the title: Who Moved the Stone? *(Byfield 1988b, 56).*

And it is clear from his column that Byfield shares the view that Christ rose bodily from the dead, just as the Bible describes.

Ted Byfield's first "Christian" Christmas

Ten years later Byfield wrote a column describing what he called his first "Christian Christmas" which occurred in 1952. Prior to that time, of course, he and his wife had celebrated Christmas as a "raucous, boozey" event. As he puts it, "those were pagan Christmases." That changed when they encountered the apologetic writings of celebrated literary scholar C. S. Lewis. Subsequently, he writes, he and Virginia "concluded that the event Christmas is supposed to commemorate had in fact occurred. It was not merely a charming story; it had *actually and literally happened*" (Byfield 1998b, 44).

Byfield explains their first exposure to C. S. Lewis this way:

> *Our initial introduction to him was a little red booklet disarmingly entitled "Broadcast Talks," the text of a wartime series on Christianity he had given over the BBC. These did not strive to establish that Christianity was psychologically sound, socially essential, or of great individual comfort, the kind of thing we had heard from pulpits whenever we couldn't escape them. No, Lewis had an entirely different aim. He sought to establish that Christianity was true, which to many people then was preposterous—indeed, outrageous. It still is (Byfield 1998b, 44).*

Lewis argued that there was indeed a Natural Law, basically moral rules that all people intuitively understand such as telling the truth and helping our families. Yet everybody breaks these rules on a regular basis. No one truly lives up to the moral code. Everyone is a sinner, in other words.

Into this world came Jesus Christ, who is both "Perfect God and perfect man," to wash away the sins of all those who will believe on Him. And the Byfields did believe.

> *After years of insipid religion, this Christ came to us like a drink of cold water in a desert. Here was a God to believe in, a faith to follow. And so we followed it that first Christian Christmas in 1952, followed it to the church and from there through the creation of schools, magazines, books, wherever it led. Of two things we can testify. We have never measured up, and we have never been bored. His mercy, as the old Jewish poet said, endures forever (Byfield 1998b, 44).*

And so it was through the apologetic writings of C. S. Lewis that the Byfields first heard the real gospel and believed in it.

Women and religion

Ted Byfield understood that there was a tight relationship between religion, politics and society in general. That would probably come across from much of his thinking presented in this book. In a column celebrating the demise of Playboy Clubs in 1988, he makes a very explicit connection between them.

Each society has a set of rules that it lives by. It cannot survive without "The Rules." In the West, the rules began to collapse during the first and second world wars. It was during that period that religion in the West deteriorated substantially and "with religion the whole basis of The Rules in North America evaporated" (Byfield 1988d, 44). Men began to think they could live without The Rules and didn't have to be strictly faithful to their wives. This laid the groundwork for the success of Hugh Hefner and his *Playboy Magazine* empire.

However, women caught on and began to realize that if men no longer had to follow The Rules, they didn't need to either. This led to the rise and success of feminism. In other words, first men rebelled against The Rules, and then women did so likewise. Feminism was one major result.

Byfield argues that because women are more central to civilization than men, feminism will lead to the downfall of Western society:

> *If a man throws over The Rules, that poses a mere problem. If a woman does, it means much deeper trouble. If all women, or most women, did it, that could promise only unparalleled catastrophe. For it is upon the woman that the whole social order always depends. She is the heart of the family which is at the heart of society. Man's sacrifices on its behalf, other than in war, are essential but light. Hers are enormous and all-embracing. If she refuses to make them, no society can survive (Byfield 1988d, 44).*

Western countries, such as Canada, are quickly abandoning The Rules that maintained them for centuries. Byfield wrote that there were three possible futures for the Western countries:

> *Societies that lose their rules are either (a) overpowered by other societies that have not lost theirs, or (b) recover their own rules through cataclysm and disaster, or (c) (if they are lucky) regain their faith through religious renewal. Out of the darkness comes a Gregory, or a Francis, or a Wesley, and we regain that which we lost. The latter, when one beholds the squalid condition of the modern church, does not seem too probable. But then again, it never has (Byfield 1988d, 44).*

Clearly, Byfield preferred a Christian revival to any of the other possibilities for the future. And he put his money where his mouth was by committing the final two decades of his life to the task of restoring Christianity in North America through a special multi-volume history of Christianity.

The Christian history series as a kind of evangelism

Ted Byfield's last major professional project was the production of a

12-volume popular history of Christianity. The final volume was completed in 2013. An important motivation for undertaking this project was the need to bring Christianity back into our culture. We have lost the Christian basis of our society and the benefits that flow from it. Our laws have been changing because most people no longer subscribe to a Christian system of morality. This will have baleful results for our country, as Byfield relates:

> You cannot expect a non-Christian society to adopt Christian-based laws, and as the liberal media never tire of telling us, we are now "pluralistic." When we fully discover what this actually means, we'll wish to heaven we weren't. A truly "pluralistic" society, having by definition no basis for its morality, must first descend into chaos, then into autocracy. That will be the short-term outcome (Byfield 2002, 60).

As a result, Byfield believes that the problems caused by the shift from Christianity to pluralism will eventually lead some people to search for "their real roots," the basis of Western society in its vibrant days.

In his view, many people no longer know how to reason properly. However, these people can be reached through a compelling narrative as well as stories and parables. But that was not all:

> Further, we realized that the liberal educators, front-runners of this disastrous revolution, had left an opening. They quit teaching history, since their aim is to produce a human being wholly enslaved by the spirit of the age, totally captive to the current fashion in everything. History, by introducing people to other ages and eras, provides them with a platform from which to view their own. So the progressives taught sociology instead and said it was history.
>
> Yet human curiosity to know where we're from, and how we got here, is impossible to kill. The educators had thus left in their program of indoctrination an unintended void—which could be our opportunity. If we could offer something to fill it, to satisfy that curiosity, and could do it with narrative, with stories, we could show a new generation the way home (Byfield 2002, 60).

So for this reason Byfield embarked upon the Christian History Project. It is an effort to show "the way home" to our Christian roots. In this sense it is a kind of evangelistic tool.

The Need for the Christian History Series

The reasons for producing the Christian History Series were very serious. Much like its evangelistic purpose, Byfield also saw it as one way of helping to turn Western society back to its roots.

Western civilization is the greatest civilization ever. It has produced the greatest good for mankind in terms of political freedom, economic prosperity, and medical technology, to mention just three major contributions. But the West has been experiencing radical changes for decades that threaten to undermine this civilization.

One important pillar of Western civilization that has been lost is its consciousness of history. Few people know how we got to where we are. To a certain degree, Byfield contends that the decreasing knowledge of history has been the deliberate outcome of the dominant philosophy of history in the twentieth century. This is not to suggest that there was some sort of "conspiracy." Rather, it is to point out that John Dewey and his movement thought they could improve society by reducing the amount of history taught in schools. But their efforts were harmful rather than beneficial.

Byfield explains:

> While the great philosopher claimed to set men free by liberating them from the "shackles" of the past, the effect was to deliver them into the bondage of the present, making them prisoners of what the Germans call the Zeitgeist, the spirit of the age. Dewey had led them to believe that the here and now, the going thing, the current style, the "acceptable" view, the latest "rage" was the only reality that existed. Thus fashion not freedom came to determine how they lived in a world where morality was a matter of "lifestyle" and truth a matter of viewpoint. They could not judge the world they lived in because they had no way to get out of it to look at it. He had locked them in. One way out was that path into the forest, so he made sure that few ever found it (Byfield 2008, 31).

If the loss of history is an important part of the problem, then it is reasonable to think that recovering a sense and knowledge of history would form part of the solution. This was the perspective that Byfield adopted, stating,

> Before we can work a change in the schools, we must set on foot a change in the culture, and popular history is the tool which can bring such a change about. Because it reflects the great values of

the past, it will work to restore the great values of the past, and the magnificent works of music, art and literature will be restored along with them. For these are among the facts and treasures of history (Byfield 2008, 34).

However, he was not so naïve as to think that this was a complete solution. Producing popular history as a means to restore Western civilization was not sufficient. But it did constitute a contribution towards the larger task. Being part of the solution was significant enough to justify the production of the Christian History Series.

What am I suggesting? That the direction of society can be changed by a set of books? No. But as the old Jewish saying goes, it's better to light one candle than complain about the dark. This series, we believe, is such a candle (Byfield 2008, 35).

In this sense the Christian History Series is part of the larger conservative project of restoring Western culture. In fact, it may become the Byfields' greatest contribution to the ongoing struggle to defend and restore the foundations of Western society.

CHAPTER 20

CONCLUSION

It is clear that genuine "small c" conservatism has a long history in western Canada. There have been numerous political leaders who reflected this perspective to one degree or another. On top of that, Link and Ted Byfield have articulated a clear conservative philosophy rooted in the culture of western Canada.

This information is not just of historical interest. If genuine conservatism is to have any sort of future in Canada, the principles represented by these leaders will need to be embraced. The free enterprise principles of Ross Thatcher, the historically-rooted Canadian patriotism of Sterling Lyon (as opposed to the Marxist-based "nationalism" promoted by leftist groups), and the social conservatism of Bill Vander Zalm must be the foundation of Canadian conservativism, at least in the West.

The political leaders recounted in the first part of the book provide clear examples of people motivated by conservatism in their objectives for government. The thought leaders in the second part of the book articulate the genuine conservative principles that need to be understood and embraced. This is the two-pronged thrust of the book: there are numerous examples of conservative political leadership in the West, and there is a conservative political philosophy from the West.

Some people will likely be more interested in the first part of the book, while others may be more interested in the second. Although both point in the same direction, it seems to me that the second part holds greater significance to the long-term health and welfare of conservatism and western Canada.

This book is not proposing a political platform for electoral success. Anyone embracing Byfield conservatism will be likely considered unelectable by the political establishment. In our current situation, people who want to be elected to office are best to embrace a mushy set of political ideals so that they can't be pinned down. This will do little to make the country better.

Canada (not to mention the other English-speaking democracies i.e., the Anglosphere) is on a steady downhill slide with no end in sight. A clear message of truth needs to be proclaimed to offer an alternative vision for the future. This vision must be rooted in historical, philosophical and spiritual reality, rather than the humanistic wishful thinking of the left-wing ideology that currently dominates Canadian culture and society.

Byfield conservatism provides just such a vision. There's no need to beat around the bush: this means that Christianity must be at the heart of any movement that aims to turn the country around.

Christianity is the key

This may be an unpleasant subject for those who consider "religion" to be distasteful and outmoded. Why not keep religion and politics separate? That way we won't unnecessarily alienate secular-minded people and other non-Christians.

What people believe about politics is a reflection of their most deeply held beliefs about life and reality. Everyone has such beliefs. Everyone has a worldview that informs their lives and behaviour. Opinions on politics flow out of people's worldviews. Every society fundamentally reflects a worldview as well. Until the last few decades, Canada's society was largely underpinned by a general Christian worldview (Wagner 2012).

Ted Byfield understood this point and it informed his own perspective and writing. In volume 3 of the Christian History Series, a contrast is made between the Roman emperors Diocletian and Constantine. Diocletian instigated the worst period of persecution of Christians under the Roman Empire. Constantine, of course, became some sort of Christian and gave Christianity a privileged place within the Empire. Byfield hints that those may be the only real options, i.e., an anti-Christian government or a pro-Christian government. A supposedly neutral government is not an option because all governments themselves are rooted in a particular worldview. If it's not a Christian worldview, it will be an alternative worldview that frowns upon Christianity.

> *Our era has come to believe in a neutral middle position called "pluralism," in which the practice of all law-abiding religions is permitted. But that concept is scarcely a hundred years old, and already we see state authority increasingly invoked to inhibit Christian activity and the expression of Christian thought. Perhaps, therefore, a coming generation will discover that there is no middle position, that the painful choice must always lie between a Constantine and a Diocletian (Byfield 2003, ix).*

Even then, having a government that is favourable towards Christianity will ultimately not be sufficient to turn the country around. It would be a big step forward, away from the kinds of policies that are running us into a ditch. But outwardly doing what's right is not enough to restore God's blessing to the land.

The real struggle

To propose an adequate solution requires an unwavering commitment to get to the root of the problem. The root of the problem is not one set of policy proposals over against another. It goes much deeper than that. As Ted Byfield wrote many years ago in response to Pierre Berton's attack upon Christianity, "the real struggle of this world is not the atomic weapons issue, nor the racial question, nor the quest for social improvement. It is the slow, vicious, deadly war between good and evil and the battleground is the heart of each man" (Byfield 1965, 149).

So here's the deal: all of us as individuals must fight that battle in our own hearts, and victory can only be won with the help of God.

The Left believes that problems in society are the result of social and economic structures. Capitalism and the traditional family are two of the sources leftists consider to be the basis of oppression and poverty. They have that completely wrong, of course. They're wrong to see people as being victims who must overthrow capitalism and traditional morality before their lives can improve.

The conservative perspective focuses much more on the individual. There are circumstances that can hamper people from flourishing in their lives. But they can still make a positive difference if they take responsibility and especially if they turn to God. The key battle for each of us is within our own hearts, not external social or economic structures.

A superficial commitment to God and Christianity will itself be insufficient. What is needed is the kind of Christianity that makes a big difference in our lives. Ted Byfield wrote about this kind of Christianity in the following inspiring passage:

> Let us hear of Christian accountants who lose big clients because they tell them the truth about the operations of their businesses. Or of Christian lawyers who live in near poverty to serve the cause of truth and justice in the courts. Or of Christian businessmen who are scorned by their colleagues because they persist in telling the truth about their products. Or of Christian labor union leaders who are driven out of office because they care about the work instead of the wage scale. Or of Christian politicians who think of leading the nation instead of following it, and are not afraid to do what is right at whatever cost to themselves, their careers, their friends and colleagues and their parties. And when we are kicked out of the club, snickered at on the street, driven into bankruptcy, fated to remain obscure, let us rejoice and be exceedingly glad. For so persecuted they those who went before us (Byfield 1965, 145).

Significant and positive change will only happen in our country when significant and positive change has happened within our own souls. We need to change ourselves first. Fundamental change cannot be expected simply from supporting and voting for conservative candidates and policies. That will never be enough.

Ironic as it might seem, fighting the battles within our own hearts while looking to God for help and guidance, is the best way to make a positive contribution to genuine conservatism. Getting our priorities right benefits us and potentially others as well. As Ted Byfield has so succinctly pointed out, "Inevitably it was those Christians who were most convinced that this world was only a means to the next one who left the greatest impression upon the affairs of this one" (Byfield 1965, 147).

REFERENCES

Alberta Views. 2008. "A Legendary Alberta Voice." June: 19.

Baron, Don, and Paul Jackson. 1991. *Battleground: The Socialist Assault on Grant Devine's Canadian Dream.* Toronto: Bedford House Publishing.

Bell, Edward. 2004. "Ernest Manning, 1943-1968." In *Alberta Premiers of the Twentieth Century.* Edited by Bradford J. Rennie. Regina: Canadian Plains Research Center.

Brennan, Brian. 2008. *The Good Steward: The Ernest C. Manning Story.* Calgary: Fifth House Ltd.

Byfield, Link. 1988. "Revolutionaries on the political horizon." *Alberta Report.* May 2: 4.

Byfield, Link. 1990. "Maybe AIDS is just the gay plague after all." *Alberta Report.* March 19: 4.

Byfield, Link. 1992. "What all gun nuts, pro-life bigots and tax rebels share: a belief in democratic freedom." *Alberta Report.* November 2: 2.

Byfield, Link. 1996a. "If parents won't force an end to school bullying, nobody else will either." *Alberta Report.* January 1: 2.

Byfield, Link. 1996b. "If Alberta's Tories think their task is finished, they should think some more." *Alberta Report.* February 12: 2.

Byfield, Link. 1996c. "Why Pat Buchanan so horrifies the North American liberal establishment." *Alberta Report.* March 4: 2.

Byfield, Link. 1996d. "Needed: Tough-minded Christians to take over the social policy of Alberta." *Alberta Report.* March 25: 2.

Byfield, Link. 1997. "How did it happen that we have no right to life, but do have a right to sodomy?" *Alberta Report.* November 17: 2.

Byfield, Link. 1998. "Albertans have to tell Ralph to give them a direct vote on gay rights." *Alberta Report.* April 27: 2.

Byfield, Link. 1999. "Our next 25 years: The battles to be fought will be harder— but like some earlier ones, they can be won." *Alberta Report.* January 11: 18-22.

Byfield, Ted. 1965. *Just Think, Mr. Berton (A Little Harder).* Winnipeg: Company of the Cross.

Byfield, Ted. 1980a. "The Montessori school case: A matter of state vs. parent." *Alberta Report.* July 18: 52.

Byfield, Ted. 1980b. "The question that got me thrown off a TV program." *Alberta Report.* July 25: 44.

Byfield, Ted. 1980c. "Lucky you, Billy Graham, you're visiting Utopia." *Alberta Report*. August 8: 44.

Byfield, Ted. 1981a. "Why entrenched educators fear the independent schools." *Alberta Report*. June 19: 52.

Byfield, Ted. 1981b. "The *Edmonton Journal's* new editor should fit right in." *Alberta Report*. August 14: 52.

Byfield, Ted. 1981c. "How Mr. Levesque may give the West a round it could win." *Alberta Report*. November 20: 60.

Byfield, Ted. 1985a. "More laws won't solve the hate problem." *Alberta Report*. October 28: 60.

Byfield, Ted. 1985b. "Introducing Western Report, an idea whose time has come." *Alberta Report*. December 9: 52.

Byfield, Ted. 1986a. "The new phony Canada is a Toronto creation." *Alberta Report*. April 14: 60.

Byfield, Ted. 1986b. "Jones lost, parents lost, but dear old P-BOG wins again." *Alberta Report*. October 20: 52.

Byfield, Ted. 1987. "Re faith: it's time you put up or shut up, Globe and Mail." *Alberta Report*. November 23: 52.

Byfield, Ted. 1988a. "The gates have been opened but the barbarian hasn't won." *Alberta Report*. February 8: 48.

Byfield, Ted. 1988b. "How, asked Mr. Berton, could the experts miss that mistake?" *Alberta Report*. April 18: 56.

Byfield, Ted. 1988c. "Why one subscriber cancelled, and why we won't repent." *Alberta Report*. July 4: 48.

Byfield, Ted. 1988d. "Farewell to the Playboy Clubs; but their sad legacy remains." *Alberta Report*. August 22: 44.

Byfield, Ted. 1988e. "Why can't the CBC leave a nice guy like me alone?" *Alberta Report*. November 7: 52.

Byfield, Ted. 1991. "The Reform party: The timing was right." In *Act of Faith: The Illustrated Chronicle of the Fastest-growing Political Movement in Canadian History: the Reform Party of Canada*. Terry O'Neill, ed. Vancouver: British Columbia Report Books. Pages 2-5.

Byfield, Ted. 1996a. "What exactly was it that gained for sodomy such a fine reputation?" *Alberta Report*. May 20: 44.

Byfield, Ted. 1996b. "Where are all the fervid champions of pluralism now that we need them?" *Alberta Report*. August 5: 44.

Byfield, Ted. 1996c. "Latest reports from the battlefront in the *Globe's* war with God." *Alberta Report*. September 2: 44.

Byfield, Ted. 1998a. "Heaven help some kids if the ideologues of the child rights brigade pull this off." *Alberta Report*. November 30: 44.

Byfield, Ted. 1998b. "Return of the Lion." *Alberta Report*. December 28: 44.

Byfield, Ted. 1999. "Well, so far so good." *Alberta Report*. January 11: 2.

Byfield, Ted. 2001. "The West's paradox—the only way we can change Canada is by finding ways to leave it." *The Report*. February 5: 60.

Byfield, Ted. 2002. "History has turned out to be highly marketable because the liberals feared to teach it." *The Report*. May 27: 60.

Byfield, Ted. 2003. "Foreword." *By This Sign A.D. 250 to 350 From the Decian Persecution to the Constantine Era*. Edmonton: The Society to Explore And Record Christian History.

Byfield, Ted. 2008. *Why History Matters: And Why Christian History Matters In Particular*. Edmonton: The Society to Explore and Record Christian History.

Carpay, John. 2002. *Revolution and Reversal: Ten Years of Premier Ralph Klein*. Edmonton: Canadian Taxpayers Federation.

Cooper, Barry. 1996. *The Klein Achievement*. Toronto: University of Toronto Centre for Public Management.

Dabbs, Frank. 1997a. *Preston Manning: The Roots of Reform*. Vancouver: Greystone Books.

Dabbs, Frank. 1997b. *Ralph Klein: A Maverick Life*. Vancouver: Greystone Books.

Davey, Keith. 1986. *The Rainmaker: A Passion for Politics*. Toronto: Stoddart Publishing.

Eisler, Dale. 2004. "Ross Thatcher." *Saskatchewan Premiers of the Twentieth Century*. Ed. Gordon L. Barnhart. Regina: Canadian Plains Research Center.

Filax, Gloria. 2006. *Queer Youth in the Province of the "Severely Normal"*. Vancouver: UBC Press.

Flanagan, Tom. 2009. *Waiting for the Wave: The Reform Party and the Conservative Movement*. Montreal & Kingston: McGill-Queen's University Press.

Flanagan, Tom. 2011. "Re: 'Has the Centre Vanished?' by Stephen Clarkson." *Literary Review of Canada*. November: 30.

Flanagan, Tom. 2013. "Legends of the Calgary School: Their Guns, Their Dogs, and the Women Who Love Them." In *Hunting and Weaving: Empiricism and Political Philosophy*. Ed. Thomas Heilke and John von Heyking. South Bend, IN: St. Augustine's Press.

Fournier, Connie. 2015. *Betrayed: Stephen Harper's War on Principled Conservatism*. Self-published.

Gunter, Lorne. 1992. "The Getty government's family defender." *Alberta Report*. July 6: 37.

Harrison, Trevor. 1995. *Of Passionate Intensity: Right-Wing Populism and the Reformed Party of Canada.* Toronto: University of Toronto Press.

Harrison, Trevor W. 2002. *Requiem for a Lightweight: Stockwell Day and Image Politics.* Montreal: Black Rose Books.

Horowitz, Gad. 1983. "Conservatism, Liberalism, and Socialism in Canada." In *Introductory Readings in Government and Politics.* Ed. Mark O. Dickerson, Thomas Flanagan and Neil Nevitte. Toronto: Methuen Publications, 126-141.

Hoy, Claire. 2000. *Stockwell Day: His Life and Politics.* Toronto: Stoddart.

Jeffrey, Brooke. 1999. *Hard Right Turn: The New Face of Neo-Conservatism in Canada.* Toronto: HarperCollins Publishers Ltd.

Lougheed, Peter. 1999. "A voice hard to ignore." *Alberta Report.* January 11: 12.

Lyon, Sterling. 1986a. "Reagan's message is Canada's reassurance." *Alberta Report.* February 24: 45.

Lyon, Sterling. 1986b. "Without Section 33 there'd be no Charter." *Alberta Report.* March 10: 57.

Macphail, Gisela. 1996. "The adverse health effects of homosexuality should be taught." *Alberta Report.* October 14: 33.

Malcolmson, John. 1984. "The Hidden Agenda of 'Restraint.'" In *The New Reality: The Politics of Restraint in British Columbia.* Eds. Warren Magnusson, William K. Carroll, Charles Doyle, Monika Langer, and R.B.J. Walker. Vancouver: New Star Books.

Moher, Frank. 1990. *Prairie Report.* Winnipeg: Blizzard Publishing, 1990.

Nicholls, Gerry. 2009. *Loyal to the Core: Stephen Harper, Me and the NCC.* St. Catharines: Freedom Press Canada.

Pitsula, James M. 2004. "Grant Devine." In *Saskatchewan Premiers of the Twentieth Century.* Edited by Gordon L. Barnhart. Regina: Canadian Plains Research Center.

Plecas, Bob. 2006. *Bill Bennett: A Mandarin's View.* Vancouver: Douglas & McIntyre.

Rovinsky, David J. 1998. *The Ascendancy of Western Canada in Canadian Policymaking.* Washington, DC: The Center for Strategic and International Studies.

Ruff, Norman. 1984. "Social Credit as Employer." In *The New Reality: The Politics of Restraint in British Columbia.* Eds. Warren Magnusson, William K. Carroll, Charles Doyle, Monika Langer, and R.B.J. Walker. Vancouver: New Star Books.

Schofield, John. 1984. "Recovery Through Restraint? The Budgets of 1983/84 and 1984/85." In *The New Reality: The Politics of Restraint in British Columbia.* Eds. Warren Magnusson, William K. Carroll, Charles Doyle, Monika Langer, and R.B.J. Walker. Vancouver: New Star Books.

Skousen, W. Cleon, and Robert N. Thompson. 1982. *Canada Can Now Adopt a Model Constitution*. Langley, BC: Omega Publications.

Spencer, Larry. 2006. *Sacrificed? Truth or Politics*. Regina: KayteeBella Productions.

Stewart, David, and Jared Wesley. 2010. "Sterling R. Lyon, 1977-1981." In *Manitoba Premiers of the 19th and 20th Centuries*. Edited by Barry Ferguson and Robert Wardhaugh. Regina: Canadian Plains Research Center.

Thompson, Robert N. 1965. *Commonsense for Canadians: A Selection of Speeches Analysing Today's Opportunities and Problems*. Toronto: McClelland and Stewart.

Thompson, Robert N. 1979. *From the Marketplace: A Christian Voice*. Langley, BC: Trinity College Press.

Thompson, Robert N. 1990. *A House of Minorities: The Political Memoirs of Robert N. Thompson*. Burlington: Welch Publishing.

Vander Zalm, Bill. 2008. *Bill Vander Zalm "For the People."* Self-published.

Wagner, Michael. 1995. "Private Versus Public Education: The Alberta Debate in the 1980s." M.A. thesis. University of Calgary.

Wagner, Michael. 2007. *Standing on Guard for Thee: The Past, Present and Future of Canada's Christian Right*. St. Catharines, ON: Freedom Press Canada.

Wagner, Michael. 2009. *Alberta: Separatism Then and Now*. St. Catharines, ON: Freedom Press Canada.

Wagner, Michael. 2012. *Leaving God Behind: The Charter of Rights and Canada's Official Rejection of Christianity*. Russell, ON: ChristianGovernance.